Cal Bombay

PRACTICAL THOUGHTS
On Paul's Letter to the

ROMANS

CROSSROADS
Family of Ministries

Published by Crossroads Christian Communications Inc.

ISBN 0-921702-78-7
Copyright 1996 Cal R. Bombay

Published by Crossroads Christian Communications Inc.
P.O. Box 5100, Burlington, Ontario, Canada L7R 4M2

CONTENTS

Introduction

The Epistle of Paul to the Church in Rome is the most powerful and complete doctrinal statement of the early Church.

The commentaries in this book are not intended to delve into the depths of every area of doctrine, nor to be exhaustive by covering every aspect of Christian faith and experience.

What I trust you will receive from these short essays is a good, practical and solid thought which will keep you thinking. For the more you think within the concept and teaching of the Scriptures, the more you will become like Jesus; and the more you become like Jesus, the stronger and longer-lasting will be your personal influence on everyone around you—that includes your family, friends, and yes, even your enemies!

My prayer is that as you ponder your way through these simple and practical teachings, that your own spirit will burst forth with praise to God who loved us enough to do the whole thing Himself. The believing is left to us!

And believing will change your life.

That is my hope.

Cal R. Bombay

Dedication
To my Friend
and Fellow Christian
Odhiambo Okite
who has taught me
Christian Endurance

Who's Talking

Romans 1:1-6

Have you ever wondered where the local pastor gets his authority to speak on behalf of God? Is it the greatness of the seminary which taught him, or the number and quality of the theological degrees after his name? Is it the backing of the denomination which makes his credentials valid? How about the evangelist or missionary? Where do they get the authority to stand up in the name of Jesus Christ and speak on God's behalf?

Several times in my experience as a minister of the Gospel, I have been shocked at the surprise on someone's face when I let them know that I am an ordained minister of the Gospel. This was usually after they had known me for at least a little while on a casual, social basis.

The usual response was: "You? You're a reverend, like in a church?" When I assure them that it is true, they normally add a few more observations, such as, "You don't act like a minister!" I then ask, "Well, what's a minister supposed to act like?"

This is when it gets interesting, because most people really don't want to reveal what they really think about the average cleric. But I get answers; answers such as "stuffy," "reserved," "quiet," and even in one case, "Well, aren't you supposed to wear special clothes or something?" I really started to feel good when one day someone said to me, "But you're so...normal!"

It's sometimes quite difficult to convince someone about your credentials. "What right do you have to preach at us?" "Who gives you the right and the authority to tell us anything?"

I'm sure it wasn't too different with the Apostle Paul. In the very beginning of his letter to the Romans, Paul dealt with that question. He had never been to Rome when he wrote to them, so they had no personal loyalty to him. It would be three years after Paul wrote this letter to Rome when he would finally arrive there, in chains. Why was he worth listening to? And what made him think he had the authority to say anything to the Romans? Paul deals with that right up front. Look at Romans 1:1-6:

> *"Paul, a bondservant of Jesus Christ, called to be an apostle, separated to the Gospel of God which He promised before through His prophets in the Holy Scriptures...."*

And with the next few words he gives a no-holds-barred statement of just who gave this authority:

> "...concerning His Son Jesus Christ our Lord, who was born of the seed of David according to the flesh, and declared to be the Son of God with power according to the Spirit of holiness, by the resurrection from the dead...."

According to the Old Testament prophets, the Christ would be of the lineage of King David. Jesus was of that lineage. You can read the whole genealogy in the Gospels. That is the fleshly line.

The spiritual proof of Jesus as the Christ was His resurrection from the dead. Such a phenomenal occurrence as coming to life again after three days in a tomb in the Middle Eastern heat could only be an act of God. Then Paul goes on to say:

> "Through Him we have received grace and apostleship for obedience to the faith among all nations for His Name, among whom you also are the called of Jesus Christ."

Paul states clearly that he is simply being obedient to a heavenly call to preach and teach the Gospel. In other words, he's saying I have the authority that only God can give to His servants.

While it is true that there are some men and women filling pulpits and performing the daily duties of a minister who may not have ever had a clear call from God into the ministry, the great majority do! God clearly places people into pastoral, teaching, prophetic and evangelistic ministries.

They should be heard, and respected, not because of their human gifts and abilities, and even less because of their personalities or good looks, but because of their call from God to serve the Church. They are God's spokesmen in an increasingly godless world. There should be expected from them an intimacy with God and with His Word. Spiritual leadership should be recognizable, as it was with the Apostle Paul.

And Paul immediately associates himself with all Christians, all the saints of God, as members of the same family of God through Jesus Christ.

Then Paul begins the greatest doctrinal treatise of the New Testament. On the following pages we will explore these great truths, found in the Book of Romans.

Saints Not Supermen

Romans 1:7-15

What do you have to do, or how do you have to act, to be thought of as a saint? Perhaps we need to examine this term "saint" to see if the way we use it today is the same as the use of that term in New Testament times. I know some saints personally who have acted like anything but saints. I also know some people who try with all their might to act like saints, but they are not—by their own admission! Sound strange? Read on!

There is a very unfortunate misconception, by many people, about religious leaders, preachers, pastors and, yes, those of us who serve God as television evangelists and teachers. Somehow or another, an aura of special greatness or holiness is attached to many Christian leaders, and alas, some even promote the idea of their own special powers with God.

The last decade should have proved to most of us that the people who inhabit the pulpit are not endued with some remarkably extra-special ability to live free from all human weakness. Each of us can bring to mind the human weakness that brought some preacher down, and which also brought great shame on the name of Jesus Christ, and His Church. No, there is nothing remarkably superhuman about any of us. We are all human, and subject to the crass and destructive foibles of all other human beings.

And this misconception of Christian leaders is even more intense when it comes to New Testament characters, such as the Apostle Paul. We call him Saint Paul, and by so doing, imply an extra-special saintliness to him. Sainthood is not a special status with God. Sainthood is the position of every single believer in Jesus Christ, no matter how weak and subject to human distortions. If a person believes in Jesus Christ as Saviour, he is a saint. He need accomplish nothing else. Sainthood is a designation of a relationship with God, not a measure of special holiness or accomplishments for God. Look at Romans 1:7:

> *"To all who are in Rome, beloved of God, called to be saints."*

Paul talks about "all" the beloved of God in Rome as "saints." Throughout the whole of the New Testament, all the Christians (or believers, or brethren), are referred to as saints. There was no special class aside. As the called of God, we are ALL called to be saints: all human, all lost in sin, all in need of a Saviour, yet all saints when we become believers and receive Jesus Christ as Lord and Master.

And, it seems to me, just to drive this point home, Paul mentions his own very human inabilities. He had wanted to come to Rome. He had even prayed about it often. Listen to Romans 1:10:

> *"My prayer...making request if, by some means, now at last I may find a way in the will of God to come to you."*

And in Romans 1:13:

> *"Now I do not want you to be unaware, brethren, that I often planned to come to you (but was hindered until now), that I might have some fruit among you also, just as among the other Gentiles."*

Isn't it amazing that an apostle, a saint of God, a powerful and very determined personality, could make plans that went awry?

You see, God does not choose superstars, necessarily, to either serve or follow Him. In fact, the Bible says in 1 Corinthians 1:27:

> *"But God has chosen the foolish things of the world to put to shame the wise, and God has chosen the weak things of the world to put to shame the things which are mighty."*

It's not necessarily the great sparkling personalities that God uses to accomplish His purposes, even though they may make a sensational impression, and draw big crowds. God seems to use the most unlikely personalities for His greatest accomplishments. Looking back in history, we may raise them to great status in our own minds, but when the actual events took place, they were just like you and me—simply saints.

And, just in case anyone thinks that Paul was writing as one Jewish Christian to the Jewish Christians in Rome, he mentions in verse 13 of this chapter that, in fact, he is writing to Gentiles.

In this book, we will be examining the truths of Romans, including the cause of something called SIN. That's not too popular a word in today's vocabulary, but it is absolutely fundamental to the understanding of the purpose and coming of Jesus Christ.

Well-Educated Fools

Romans 1:16-25

When I lived in Africa, I wrote a little paper under my nom-de-plume, Richard Kihara, entitled, "Even Educated People Die." Literally millions of people read it, in many languages. WHY? Because it dealt with two very fundamental questions: "Why doesn't education, science and technology ever seem to provide real and lasting answers? And why, no matter how wealthy you may get, does the end of human experience still end up hollow, and in death?"

The most fundamental fault in our society is its reluctance to take into account the nature of man when dealing with mankind's problems. We have social programs designed around almost every social theory in existence, feebly pecking away at the monstrous problems in society. And while we inch forward to the utopian perfection we dream of, at the same time we slide back even further. We are not gaining ground that was promised by the theorists, in spite of their research and conclusions, in spite of the sciences and technology. Human problems seem to increase in this modern world, rather than decrease!

Psychiatrists and psychologists can often bring the problems to light for more clear definition, but seldom can they give the permanent help people need. Often years of therapy are used up with little effect. And if that's not true, then why do the clients keep going back—for years? Oh, I'm not saying it never helps to talk things through. It certainly does. But until society is ready to admit there is an element in human nature which cannot be ignored any longer, we will have few successes and few advances.

But, immediately, someone could say, "That sounds like a preacher just sounding off." Well, stop and think for a moment. If preachers represent God, as they claim, (and it's true that God made us all), isn't it possible that God's Word might have something valuable to say about human nature? And isn't it possible that some preacher might quote something from God's Word that, in fact, does speak to the problems of men? Isn't it possible that man's salvation could come from God? In Romans 1:16, Paul writes:

> *"For I am not ashamed of the Gospel of Christ, for it is the power of God to salvation for everyone who believes...."*

The salvation of the human race is possible only through God, its Creator. And God has chosen to send His own Son to show the way. The Bible goes on, in the most clear, and powerful way, in Romans 1:18 saying:

"For the wrath of God is revealed from heaven against all ungodliness and unrighteousness of men, who suppress the truth in unrighteousness because what may be known of God is manifest in them, for God has shown it to them. For since the creation of the world His invisible attributes are clearly seen, being understood by the things that are made, even His eternal power and Godhead, so that they are without excuse, because, although they knew God, they did not glorify Him as God, nor were thankful, but became futile in their thoughts, and their foolish hearts were darkened."

It is in the nature of man to know God. Evidence of God is all around us. The human heart, even the most depraved, has a little reserved area that, when in despair, whimpers out to God. But man is a proud creature: "I can make it!" "I have been adequately educated to handle life." There is a great reluctance to accept any other opinion than my own. My opinion is better than any other opinion, even God's. And then we read a simple fact, in Romans 1:22:

"Professing to be wise, they became fools."

So man goes his own way, tries all his own theories, makes advances in science and technology, and forms a better and better opinion of himself. And when he is faced with tragedy, a dilemma, a personal crisis that science and technology doesn't even speak to, he still thinks he can handle the internal matters of the soul on his own. So God leaves people on their own—wallowing in their own godless wisdom. Look at Romans 1:24:

"Therefore God also gave them up to uncleanness, in the lusts of their hearts, to dishonour their bodies among themselves."

We will be taking a closer look at the basic nature of man in the next few studies. We'll tell it like it is. We'll find out what the Bible means when it says, in verse 21 "...their foolish hearts were darkened!"

Darkness breeds all kinds of evil. Yet the light dispels darkness. And as the Bible itself says, the "Word of God is a light to our pathway." Join me in the following chapters as we journey on this well-lighted path.

The Debased Human Mind
Romans 1:26-32

When is sin really not sin? We have a few dozen opinions loose in our confused world as to what constitutes sin, or even whether or not there is such a thing as "sin." What do you think? What do I think? Well, as a matter of fact, I've decided to take Someone else's Word for it, because there is a strong possibility my own mind could be off base on this one. Don't feel so smug! You might just be off base, too! The Bible, God's Word, will enlighten our minds on this important matter.

Verbal storms rage around the issue of sin. There are those who are quick to condemn anyone who lives in a way that they don't agree with. They imagine some things are sins which will condemn the person doing it to total damnation. They may even be able to string off a whole list of unrighteous acts, and even thoughts, that are sure to send someone else to hell.

On the other hand, there are those who would like to eradicate the very thought of sin, and to say that someone has committed a sin is to heap unnecessary guilt on an already poor self-image. So, who is right? Or, is there a middle ground?

Well, the Bible has some pretty clear definitions both of what sin is, and what its results are. First, look at what it says in 1 John 5:17:

> *"All unrighteousness is sin, and there is sin not leading to death."*

All unrighteousness is sin. That is a firm and irrevocable statement from God's Word. But the second part of that verse says that there is such a thing as sin that doesn't have an eternal death penalty. So, our question is, how can we be sure of the difference? Well, let's read Romans 1:26-28:

> *"For this reason* (because they forsook God's truth - see verse 25) *God gave them up to vile passions. For even their women exchanged the natural use for what is against nature. Likewise also the men, leaving the natural use of the woman, burned in their lust for one another, men with men committing what is shameful, and receiving in themselves the penalty of their error which was due. And even as they did not like to retain God in their knowledge, God gave them over to a debased mind, to do those things which are not fitting...."*

The sexual perversions described here are sins. But they are not the only sins. In the next few verses are listed over twenty other sins, all of them worthy of eternal death. Look at Romans 1:32:

> *"...knowing the righteous judgment of God, that those who practice such things are deserving of death, not only do the same but also approve of those who practice them."*

Those who do all these things, according to the Bible, are guilty, and the penalty is death; eternal separation from God.

We will deal with the matter of guilt in a later study.

At this point, we want to point out that sin, the kind which is worthy of death, separates men from God. It leaves men in darkness, away from the light of God. It puts man under God's judgment. Man's judgment is almost irrelevant in these matters. The best we can do is simply point out what the Bible says is God's judgment on these things.

We can also point out what the Bible says we can do about it. Later in this same book of Romans, in 6:13 we read:

> *"And do not present your members as instruments of unrighteousness to sin, but present yourselves to God as being alive from the dead, and your members as instruments of righteousness to God."*

The choice is yours. You choose whether to live in sin or not to live in sin. In verse 32, we see that it's those who practice these sins who are worthy of death. What then, if someone stops practicing, or living in these kinds of sins?

The way out from under the weight, the habit and guilt of these sins is really rather simple. As this verse says, you present yourself, with all your parts and pieces, to God, as instruments of righteousness. And, do as the Bible says in 1 John 1:9:

> *"If we confess our sins, He is faithful and just to forgive us our sins and to cleanse us from all unrighteousness."*

He can cleanse us from all unrighteousness. Not just the unrighteousness of the other fellow, but the ones of which you and I are also guilty. More about that in the next study. As you can see, the Apostle Paul is dealing with some very basic problems in human nature, and the very basics of the Christian faith.

God, The Judge

Romans 2:1-11

Some very over-publicized court cases were before the judges over a long period of time. Both the O.J. Simpson trial and the Paul Bernardo trial have been sensationalised to the point that you wonder how a judge and jury could ever be totally impartial. And with the added factors of influence and cold hard cash, you could wonder if the public ever did really hear and know the truth. Question: Can a judge be 100% impartial?

Passing judgment in some of the cases before the courts these days must be a harrowing experience for the judge. The jury, too, must have had some second and third thoughts about what is true or false. Guilt is difficult to determine, especially in an age when we have arrived at the point where we decide on "degrees of guilt." If guilty, how guilty? Does anyone else share the guilt?

In the second chapter of Romans, after reading of some very specific sins (a sin is a crime against God's Laws), most of us could quickly assign guilt to someone in our circle of knowledge who is clearly guilty of one of these sins. If you doubt this, read Romans chapter one again, and think for awhile. Yet, when we come to chapter two of Romans, we are brought up rather short. Read Romans 2:2-4 with me:

> *"But we know that the judgment of God is according to truth against those who practice such things."*

Of course, even God would find them guilty. And we'd probably think of ourselves as not guilty. But the Bible continues:

> *"And do you think this, O man, you who judge those practicing such things, and doing the same, that you will escape the judgment of God? Or do you despise the riches of His goodness, forbearance, and longsuffering, not knowing that the goodness of God leads you to repentance?"*

What the Scripture is saying here is that none of us is in a position to judge others for any sin, since every single one of us is a guilty sinner. The difference between Christians and non-Christians is not that one lot is sinless, and the other is sinful. The difference between Christians and non-Christians is described later in Romans. So, we see that God is the only One with a clear enough knowledge of both truth and the facts, to pass judgment. But how does He do this? Let us now read Romans 2:6-8:

"God...who will render to each one according to his deeds: eternal life to those who by patient continuance in doing good seek for glory, honour, and immortality; but to those who are self-seeking and do not obey the truth, but obey unrighteousness—indignation and wrath."

At first glance, we might think that Paul is promoting an escape from unrighteousness, through decisive action to do good. That is not the case! In these verses he's simply making it clear that sin, wickedness, and evil will be judged by God, and that this thing called sin has totally permeated the whole human race. That leaves none of us qualified to judge and condemn someone else.

Later in this letter he deals very extensively with how to become righteous. Here he is saying sin will be judged according to the way we live. Later he will show the reason that some live in sin, and others live in righteousness, and that the relationship with God by faith is more crucial than our self-righteous efforts.

It's made very clear in John 3:36:

"He who believes in the Son has everlasting life; and he who does not believe the Son shall not see life, but the wrath of God abides on him."

In these early verses of Romans, we find that every person on earth is a guilty sinner, and that none of us has the right or the authority to determine another person's eternal destiny. We are all sinners, we will all face God. It says in Romans 2:11:

"For there is no partiality with God."

There is a key word in verse four that we'll get to later. It is "repentance." But at this point—face it—we will all face God for ourselves some day!

Next, we'll consider God's rules, which define sin, and apply to the whole human race.

Laws Are Also For The Ignorant

Romans 2:12-16

In North America, we live under a system of law. Laws govern our society, and provide parameters for the behaviour of every citizen. You can smoke cigarettes and ruin your lungs, but you can't force someone else to smoke. We have both liberty and law. The laws are designed for the good of all society. But you'll be punished for breaking one of these laws, even if you didn't know you were a lawbreaker. Does that make the law unfair? No! It just makes the law universal.

There are very few people other than lawyers who have read all the laws which are currently in effect here in Canada. There are federal laws, provincial laws and municipal laws. The full body of the law is a large collection of books. Not everyone knows the law.

A young man had just discovered a great fishing hole. He went there often and always caught his limit. He had to walk through a great deal of bush to get there, but it was worth it to catch his limit every time. He did not know that a road came within fifty yards of this favourite fishing hole, and that he could have saved himself miles of hard walking through the bush. Something else he didn't know was that off the main road there was a sign saying, "NO FISH-ING."

One day, with his near limit on the shore beside him, he was arrested and charged under the law. He pled, "I didn't know! I didn't see any signs! Nobody told me—please—I'm innocent!" Innocent? The fact is, he broke the law! He may have been ignorant of the law, but still, before the cold hard facts of the law, he was guilty. The classic phrase is, "Ignorance is no excuse!"

With that in mind, let's look at Romans 2:12-14:

> *"For as many as have sinned without Law will also perish without Law, and as many as have sinned in the Law will be judged by the Law...."*

Please notice it says those who have sinned, with a knowledge of the Law, or even without a knowledge of the Law, will be judged. It's the sinning which brings the judgment, not the knowledge of the Law. Let's read on:

> *"...for not the hearers of the Law are just in the sight of God, but the doers of the Law will be justified; for when Gentiles, who do not have*

the Law, by nature do the things in the Law, these, although not having the Law, are a law to themselves...."

The Jews had the Law. If they broke it, they sinned, and they knew it. The Gentiles by their very nature knew murder, theft and adultery were wrong. There is some built-in understanding of right and wrong, in the very core of our nature. Doing wrong is a universal behaviour. Later, we see this fact clarified even more, in Romans 3:23:

"...for all have sinned and fall short of the glory of God."

Although God's Law was not known by all men in its revealed clarity, the fact of sin was recognized by even the most godless conscience.

But then we have a dilemma. Can the Law make anyone just and righteous? The fact of the matter is that the best it can do is show how sinful we really are. For, just as the laws of Canada are in the thousands, so are the Laws of God. They cover more than murder, theft and adultery. To keep all of them at all times is not really possible.

We must be very honest with ourselves when studying God's Word. Otherwise, looking at one Scripture, or even a few in isolation, can lead to wrong doctrine. The whole of Scripture, just like the whole of Romans, must be taken together. Paul is slowly and carefully building his case in Romans. Look with me now at James 2:10 where we read:

"For whoever shall keep the whole Law, and yet stumble in one point, he is guilty of all."

And then Paul again, still writing on this same truth in Galatians 2:16 says:

"...knowing that a man is not justified by the works of the Law but by faith in Jesus Christ, even we have believed in Christ Jesus, that we might be justified by faith in Christ and not by the works of the Law; for by the works of the Law no flesh shall be justified."

The Law, though good, just doesn't quite hack it. So whether or not you have had the advantage of the written Laws of God hardly makes a difference, unless it deepens the guilt of those who did know the Law. Ignorance of the Law is no excuse, and as we will see in our next study, being a Jew wasn't enough either. We've come across the word "righteous" several times already in Romans. In our next study, we'll find out exactly what it means.

Righteousness - What Is It?

Romans 1,2 and 3

Wouldn't it be great to be right all the time? Of course there are some people who think they are. You've met them. Their opinion is superior to yours. And to find out, you don't usually even have to ask them. They're right up front with their rightness. But they do rather make you sick, don't they? They always have the answer; always are the first to let you know their opinion. But you and I know better, don't we? You and I know that no one is right all the time, because—we know ourselves.

Since we began this study in Romans, we have already come across the word "righteous." We will see it many more times in the next few chapters. We must fully understand what the word really means if we are going to understand the letter to the Romans. And, our understanding of this word must be in the context of the Scriptures, not just current usage. The first use of this word was when Paul mentions the Gospel, and in Romans 1:17. He talks about God's righteousness:

> *"For in it the righteousness of God is revealed from faith to faith; as it is written, 'The just shall live by faith.'"*

Then in both Romans 1:32, and 2:5, we see the phrase... *"the righteous judgment of God."*

Righteousness simply means "right-ness." Having the quality and the ability to do the right thing under each and every circumstance. It is an internal, innate quality which controls the outward actions, all decisions, and even thought. This is the quality God wants all men everywhere to have. To be able, by very nature, to do the right thing under all circumstances. So when we refer to the "righteous judgment of God," we understand that He will always do the right things and make the right judgment in each and every situation. For God is always "right." And obviously, since God is always right, it is His righteousness which should always be considered standard, and "most right."

But righteousness is not just something we "do," but something we "are." Jesus spoke of this when He said to the Pharisees in Matthew 23:28-29:

> *"Even so you also outwardly appear righteous to men, but inside you are full of hypocrisy and lawlessness. Woe to you, scribes and Pharisees, hypocrites! Because you build the tombs of the prophets and adorn the monuments of the righteous...."*

Their "righteousness" was just a public act, but in their hearts and in their own

23

homes they were something else. And this was the case, simply because they were not righteous inside, where it counts. That is precisely why Jesus said in John 7:24:

> *"Do not judge according to appearance, but judge with righteous judgment."*

So when we make our judgments of right and wrong, we have two sources of reference, in knowing what is right or wrong: 1) Our very nature and conscience tells us the basics, and 2) the Laws of God as they were revealed to God's chosen people which provide the more precise definitions of what is right and what is wrong. The Law never provided righteousness, it simply defined it and demanded it. Look at Romans 3:20:

> *"Therefore by the deeds of the Law no flesh will be justified in His sight, for by the Law is the knowledge of sin."*

In Galatians, we see an expansion of this truth. Look at Galatians 2:16:

> *"...knowing that a man is not justified by the works of the Law but by faith in Jesus Christ, even we have believed in Christ Jesus, that we might be justified by faith in Christ and not by the works of the Law; for by the works of the Law no flesh shall be justified."*

The Law does not provide righteousness, it merely demands it. Jesus actually provides righteousness, and it is simply by believing the Gospel. Righteousness comes by faith. In Romans 4:3 we see this illustrated by Paul quoting from the Old testament. Listen to what he writes:

> *"For what does the Scripture say? 'Abraham believed God, and it was accounted to him for righteousness.'"*

So righteousness comes from the inside, to the outside, into our actions, decisions and even attitudes. It is not just like a coat that you put on when it's convenient.

Any unrighteousness is sin. Pure righteousness is found only in God. He, therefore, is the only One who can rightly judge any of us. And during revival, when the Holy Spirit is at work, that is precisely what happens. Great and deep conviction comes into people's hearts, and they are moved toward God, in repentance.

Oh God, pour out your Spirit upon us!

More On Righteousness

Romans 1 and 6

It's a funny thing about being lost in the woods. You never know you're lost, until suddenly you find out that you are! Starting out on the path through the woods provides confidence. Others have gone before, otherwise, why would the path be there? Right? And everything seems fine until you come to a crossroads or something very interesting or enticing off the path. Thrashing through the woods looking for the right path can be a terrifying experience—especially if you catch sight of a bunch of skeletons just ahead. Read on, we're going to try to keep you "on track."

The original meaning of the word righteous, was to "move in a straight line." To get from one place to another, the best and most efficient way, is a straight line. Any deviation from the straight line is to slow down the process, and to make the trip less efficient. Thus, when God created man, he created him perfectly, to walk in the right way; to live in the best, most comfortable, and most effective way. That was called "righteousness." To go any other way is to 'step out of line.'

Now, the opposite to righteousness (or walking in a straight path), is unrighteousness (or walking a crooked path). The Laws of God were precise about walking in the straight line; the right way, or, "righteously." As an example, let's look at a simple Law from Deuteronomy 25:15-16:

> *"You shall have a perfect and just weight, a perfect and just measure, that your days may be lengthened in the land which the Lord your God is giving you. For all who do such things, all who behave unrighteously, are an abomination to the Lord your God."*

God promises long life to those who are honest; those who are "straight" in their dealings with others, and He expresses how obnoxious to Him are those who are not straight and honest; those who are unrighteous. Back in Romans 1:29 we see the beginning of a list of things defined as off track, or unrighteous. Read it:

> *"...being filled with all unrighteousness, sexual immorality, wickedness, covetousness, maliciousness; full of envy, murder, strife, deceit, evil-mindedness; they are whisperers...."*

That could become a long list if Paul had desired to be exhaustive. But any one of us can supply a list of things that people do that are crooked, or unrighteous; things that are not a part of God's original plan for man's walk through life. The most exhaustive list is contained in the Old Testament Laws.

The Apostle Peter describes what has happened to mankind, and those who lead others off the path in particular, in 2 Peter 2:15:

> *"They have forsaken the right way and gone astray, following the way of Balaam the son of Beor, who loved the wages of unrighteousness."*

It may seem the wages are better or the returns are better the crooked way, but, I assure you, that is extremely temporary. This thing called unrighteousness is also called sin in the Bible. And the returns, or the wages, are mentioned in Romans 6:13 and 23:

> *"And do not present your members as instruments of unrighteousness to sin, but present yourselves to God as being alive from the dead, and your members as instruments of righteousness to God."*

> *"The wages of sin is death...."*

But death was not God's plan for man. That's why He sent Jesus, His Son, and our Saviour, who said, in John 14:6:

> *"I am the way, the truth, and the life. No one comes to the Father except through Me."*

Jesus came to bring people back to the straight path. He is the way. He invites all men, everywhere to get back on track. Mankind has wandered so far off the "straight line"—away from God's intended design for life—that they can't find their way back; no matter how hard they try and no matter how many different religions they invent to try to provide the "straight way" again. That's why Jesus said, "No one comes to the Father except through Me!"

The invitation to stop living in the crooked, deviated way has always been offered by God. The prophet Isaiah was one who spoke for God, when he said in Isaiah 55:7:

> *"Let the wicked forsake his way, and the unrighteous man his thoughts; let him return to the Lord, and He will have mercy on him; and to our God, for He will abundantly pardon."*

If you look inside yourself, and are honest, you'll find unrighteousness. But, if you think you're alright, and are pretty successful in walking a straight line, I think you better get ready for Romans 2:17-29 in our next study, even if you're not a Jew.

Works Don't Work

Romans 2:17-29

Can you imagine spending your whole life doing what you thought was right, only to find out that it was all wrong? It's like communism. In theory, it was supposed to change the world! But after 74 years, it collapsed, and millions of lives were thrown into confusion. But rather than admit the wrong and change, some want to bring back that old system, just because it had at least some semblance of order. Have you ever felt like that? Something in your life you thought would work isn't working? I might just be able to help you.

The apostle Paul was a Jew. For many years, he felt that his Jewishness gave him an advantage over everyone else in the world. And He worked like crazy to show how committed he was to the Laws of God. He was so convinced that these Laws were the most clear and best insights into God and godliness, that he was willing to go on a rampage of hate and murder to wipe out Christians. In other words, he was willing to condone murder, which was against the very Laws he thought he was serving. Then God arrested him.

Can you imagine how hard it was for Paul to write these words that we find in Romans 2:17-21:

> *"Indeed you are called a Jew, and rest on the Law, and make your boast in God, and know His will, and approve the things that are excellent, being instructed out of the Law, and are confident that you yourself are a guide to the blind, a light to those who are in darkness, an instructor of the foolish, a teacher of babes, having the form of knowledge and truth in the Law. You, therefore, who teach another, do you not teach yourself? You who preach that a man should not steal, do you steal?"*

And he mentioned a few other things that are against the Law, such as adultery and idolatry. And you can add the whole list of wrongs that men do. Dishonesty, hate, murder—the whole lot. Paul was there. He had been in exactly the position he was now pointing out to the Jews of that day who were so proud of their Law, yet so guilty of breaching the Law themselves. He goes on to say in Romans 2:23:

> *"You who make your boast in the Law, do you dishonour God through breaking the Law?"*

A Jew is a person who accepts the Laws as God gave them to Moses, and who is, at least in theory, committed to living according to those Laws. Yet for all the visible adherence to the Law, the hearts of the Jews of Paul's day were far from God. They boasted about their Jewishness. So Paul tells them in no uncertain terms, that for all their outward perfection, many Gentiles acted better than Jews, even though they didn't have the advantage of the Law. Listen to Romans 2:28-29:

"For he is not a Jew who is one outwardly, nor is circumcision that which is outward in the flesh; but he is a Jew who is one inwardly; and circumcision is that of the heart, in the Spirit, not in the letter; whose praise is not from men but from God."

This is the crux of the matter: the heart and the Spirit. What we really are, and what we really believe, is deep inside us. We can put on a pretty good show for a while, and deceive a lot of people. The old saying goes, "You can fool a lot of people a lot of the time, but you can't fool all the people, all the time." That's probably true, but there is something that I am absolutely convinced is true, and that is this: "You can never fool God!"

Jesus pointed out the same thing when He quoted the prophet Isaiah, in Matthew 15:8:

"These people draw near to Me with their mouth, and honour Me with their lips, but their heart is far from Me."

They are off the straight path. Although they have their own deviations, their own crooked places, and work as hard as they can to appear righteous, they can't get it past God's penetrating gaze. He knows! He sees! When the prophet Samuel was trying to make the choice of who would be king over Israel, He was brought up short by God for simply accepting appearance. We read, in 1 Samuel 16:7:

"The Lord does not see as man sees; for man looks at the outward appearance, but the Lord looks at the heart."

In Isaiah 64:6, he says this about all our hard work at looking good:

"All our righteousnesses are like filthy rags."

That should tell us that works don't work. Then the content of our next study is obvious. If works don't work, what does work?

Believe It Or Not

Romans 3:1-9

When I lived in Africa, it was very apparent that each tribe considered itself superior, in more than one way, to any neighbouring tribe. In fact, a form of insult to a person of your own tribe was to compare him to another tribe. But that thought pattern is not exclusive to Africa. Try it on yourself! It fits, doesn't it? We all think we have a slight edge over any other ethnic group. Like the age-old difference between the Jews and the Gentiles. Is there any advantage to being either one or the other?

Is there an advantage to being a Jew? You certainly wouldn't think so the way they have been treated over the centuries. Never has a people been more oppressed, enslaved and decimated by persecution than the Jewish people. So what could there possibly be as an advantage in being a Jew?

Quite simply, they had the advantage of the Laws and Ordinances of God spelled out for them. God chose them as an example of a people who could show the rest of the world what it meant to live the way God expected man to live. Look at Romans 3:1-2:

> *"What advantage then has the Jew, or what is the profit of circumcision? Much in every way! Chiefly because to them were committed the oracles of God."*

Now, just because everyone throughout the tribes of Israel didn't necessarily believe and obey the Laws and Ordinances of God, that didn't make the Law any less the "Law." The Law still stood, even though everyone may have broken it! God's Laws stand firm. They do not change with the tide of human opinion. God is sovereign.

And it's the same today! Just because the majority in society choose to disobey God, that doesn't change God's mind or will. God will remain faithful to His Word and Will. Even if up to 100% of society decide to vote in favour of adultery, or murder, or some sexual perversion, in God's eyes, it's still sin. Look at Romans 3:3:

> *"For what if some did not believe? Will their unbelief make the faithfulness of God without effect?"*

So we find that everyone, whether Jew or Gentile, will be judged by the Law! Some might cry, "Unfair! Unfair! How can God judge Gentiles on the same basis as the Jews, who had the advantage of the clearly revealed Laws and

Ordinances of God? How can God be so unfair?" Now look at Romans 3:5-6:

"But if our unrighteousness demonstrates the righteousness of God, what shall we say? Is God unjust who inflicts wrath? (I speak as a man). Certainly not! For then how will God judge the world?"

Two things which are important to remember: 1) Everyone is born with an innate sense of right and wrong, yet does wrong, and 2) God is sovereign! Never underestimate the power, authority and omnipotence of God. He is God! He will do as He sees fit! And if God says that all men live with the principle of sin embedded in them from birth, then who's to argue? Especially when God offers such a clear and clean escape from that sin principle so that we don't have to live in sin anymore. If God offers us deliverance from sin through simple belief, or faith, who are we to insist that we have any kind of alternative plan?

So the Apostle Paul, even though a Jew himself, makes it clear that the Gospel supersedes the Laws as contained in the ordinances, and brings all men, of any and every origin, into obligation to the Gospel of Jesus Christ. The Jews, in this, have no advantage over the Gentiles. Look at Romans 3:9:

"What then? Are we better than they? Not at all. For we have previously charged both Jews and Greeks (Gentiles) that they are all under sin."

And that's why none of us is in a position to judge others regarding their personal relationship to God. Oh, yes! The Bible says that the elders have an obligation to judge and assess in spiritual matters within the church, such as in 1 Corinthians 14:29:

"Let two or three prophets speak, and let the others judge."

So we find that God's judgment, which is totally impartial, puts every man, woman, and child in the world in a state of sin. That is why the Gospel of the Lord Jesus Christ is universal. This is not some local tribal religion. This is God's provision for the whole world.

It worked for the Philippian jailer 2000 years ago (Acts 16), as well as for the Roman governor. And it works for the 20th century Canadian right now. You need only believe in, and receive the Lord Jesus Christ as your own personal Saviour.

Fruitless Search

Romans 3:9-20

Marriage is starting to get very popular again. Our national magazines have reported a recent upsurge in commitment to family life, and marriage for life. That's great! I like it! I believe in it! But there still seems to be a flaw in our expectations. All the prospective brides and grooms are looking for the perfect mate—even though every one of them will admit themselves not to be perfect. Yet they keep hoping to meet the "perfect" one. Sorry, there ain't no such animal! I'll tell you why!

We've all heard about the young man who was looking for the perfect bride! She had to be beautiful, a pleasant personality, and a fabulous cook. And, she had to have the happy willingness to put up with all his imperfections! Then, of course, the young lady is looking for the tall, dark, handsome, rich and ever-giving groom. Well, if you are in your teens, and have such hopes, I've got news for you: It ain't gonna happen!

Every religion I have ever studied has the deep-rooted sense or conviction that humanity is not good enough. And all religions have been formed around the universal conviction that we somehow have got to be better than we are. So, rules, regulations, laws and ordinances are put in place to try to produce better human behaviour. Yet, no one quite seems to make it! The search for the perfect man or woman has been fruitless. Look at what is quoted from the Psalms, in Romans 3:10-13:

> *"As it is written: 'There is none righteous, no, not one; there is none who understands; there is none who seeks after God. They have all turned aside; they have together become unprofitable; there is none who does good, no, not one.'"*

Mankind has turned to his own devices, and even invented his own gods and his own world view, rather than looking to God the Creator, and obeying His Laws. Look again at Romans 3:18:

> *"There is no fear of God before their eyes."*

And even in spite of the Laws which came directly from God for the good of mankind, man, in arrogant pride, looks for his own path to perfection. Almost 3000 years ago, one of God's prophets pointed this out. Look at Isaiah 53:6:

> *"All we like sheep have gone astray; we have turned, every one, to his own way; and the Lord has laid on Him the iniquity of us all."*

This departure from the right way, God's ways (which is called righteousness) is both universal, and consistent throughout all the generations of all mankind. And the attempts at making corrective laws has also been universal through all time. The worst of it is, that the failure to keep the laws, to become better, to improve the human condition, has also been universal through all time. And, the most awesome realization of all is that, even the Laws which God Himself gave failed to produce one perfect human being! Look now at Romans 3:20:

> *"Therefore by the deeds of the Law no flesh will be justified in His sight, for by the Law is the knowledge of sin."*

Now that is an interesting statement, "...for by the Law is the knowledge of sin." It is the Law that makes sin recognizable. Now, when it comes to the word "sin," a lot of people get really uncomfortable. Sin has deep implications with spiritual and eternal overtones. No one really likes to admit to sin. We'd much rather call it mistakes, failures, shortcomings, or even wrong-doings. But sin! Somehow that brings God into it! So men, universally, look to themselves to find out what is best: "If it feels good, do it!" "I'm the master of my own fate!" But look at what the Bible says in Deuteronomy 12:8:

> *"You shall not at all do as we are doing here today—every man doing whatever is right in his own eyes."*

Our own ways don't work. God has a design for our living. The best of life, and the greatest fulfilment comes when we go God's way. It's foolish to try to invent a way that is better than God's design for our living. God's Laws are for our good. Disobedience to God's Laws brings its own consequences: often, physical death, and in the long range, spiritual death! Look at Proverbs 12:15:

> *"The way of a fool is right in his own eyes, but he who heeds counsel is wise."*

And what better counsel to take, than God's own Word. Jesus said, in Matthew 11:28:

> *"Come to Me, all you who labour and are heavy laden, and I will give you rest."*

If you're not sure what that means, just take the following steps:

1. Acknowledge that you are a sinner (Romans 3:23).
2. Confess that you cannot save yourself (Ephesians 2:8,9).
3. Realize that Jesus is the only One who can forgive you (John 14:6).
4. Confess with your mouth that Jesus is your Lord; believe that God raised Him from the dead (Romans 10:9).
5. Now, accept God's invitation to join His family (John 1:12).

The Only Alternative

Romans 3:21-26

My brother-in-law, Fred Mott, is an expert in furniture building, furniture finishes, and building, generally. He teaches at Conestoga College in Kitchener. But he ran into a problem when renovating his own kitchen at home. He tried everything under the sun, it seemed, to remove some old tile adhesive. My sister Lois was probably pretty tired of all the smells of the different solvents Fred tried to dissolve that super-resistant stuff— and in her kitchen too! Then one day, Fred had a flash of genius. Here's what he did:

At my sister's request, Fred was busy renovating the kitchen in an older house he and Lois had bought. This involved stripping some old tiles from a wall, and getting it down to a smooth surface. The compound that had held the tiles to the wall was all bumpy, and as hard as stone. He tried everything to break down that adhesive compound. He tried paint thinner. It didn't work. He tried an acid. It didn't work. He scouted the shelves of the hardware stores, trying several guaranteed products. None of them worked. Then one day, he came to the conclusion, there was only one alternative left that he had not tried. Water! Just simple, plain, ordinary, available everywhere—water! And it worked. The compound immediately softened, dissolved, and came away, leaving a smooth clean surface.

All the man-made stuff didn't work. The use of simple, original, water (which God made) worked. Good old water!

There is a similarity here. Man has tried all kinds of solutions to counteract the fact of evil—to take the hard and lumpy things out of our lives when trying to end up with a smooth and clean life. Religions, philosophies and belief systems have been invented by the genius of the human mind for centuries. In theory, some of them really look like they should work. But they don't! And so this creation was left with only one alternative, the Creator's solution: water! The water of life. Look at Romans 3:21-23:

> *"But now the righteousness of God apart from the Law is revealed, being witnessed by the Law and the Prophets, even the righteousness of God, through faith in Jesus Christ, to all and on all who believe. For there is no difference; for all have sinned and fall short of the glory of God."*

The Old Testament, both the Law and the Prophets, stands as a monument to the fact that man's solutions do not quite work. And God's answer, in Jesus Christ, is the only alternative; not just to the Jews who witnessed the failure of the Law in bringing about true righteousness, but also to the Gentiles with all their religious solutions as well. All have sinned! All need the lumpy hardness of sin removed. All need the free water of life. Look at Romans 3:24-26:

> *"Being justified freely by His grace through the redemption that is in Christ Jesus, whom God set forth as a propitiation by His blood, through faith, to demonstrate His righteousness...."*

Propitiation simply means appeasement. God's own justice demands that sin be punished, and God, in grace, freely offered His own Son, Jesus Christ, to be the appeasement to the demands of His own justice, by taking your sins, and mine, on Himself. Let us read on:

> *"...because in His forbearance God had passed over the sins that were previously committed, to demonstrate at the present time His righteousness, that He might be just and the Justifier of the one who has faith in Jesus."*

So our faith, in the simple provision of God, in Jesus Christ is like switching from all the man-made products that my brother-in-law repeatedly tried. They all failed, until he tried the simple, free and original solution: water. It worked almost like a miracle after all the other guaranteed stuff. And it was free!

Jesus talked about the water of life in John 4:14. He said:

> *"...but whoever drinks of the water that I shall give him will never thirst. But the water that I shall give him will become in him a fountain of water springing up into everlasting life."*

If you have never tried the water of life, which only God can provide, freely, there is an invitation, from the Spirit of God, and from all of us who belong to the Church of Jesus Christ, the Bride of Christ. Note Revelation 22:17:

> *"And the Spirit and the Bride say, 'Come!' And let him who hears say, 'Come!' And let him who thirsts come. Whoever desires, let him take the water of life freely."*

It doesn't matter what your religious background, the Gospel is for you! It's free, and it's the only alternative!

The New Law Called "Faith"!

Romans 3:27-31

When I bought some experienced laying hens from a local farmer, I did not realize I was buying them out of slavery. They had been confined in very small cages, and didn't know how to handle the liberty they suddenly had received. They huddled on the floor, without enough faith to stand up and walk around until some of my older chickens—more experienced in liberty—were able to help them. Yet with all this new-found freedom, they were still subject to the laws of nature.

I have chickens which are enjoying a new liberty. They used to belong to a chicken farm where several hens were confined in small cages. They ate, slept, laid eggs, drank and fully existed in total confinement: hundreds of little crowded cages.

When I bought them, I set them loose in my barn with access to the barnyard. They didn't know how to handle this new liberty. They were free to go anywhere they wanted, but they remained squatting on the floor, until some of my older chickens illustrated the freedom they had been given. Slowly, but surely, they began to move about, and to enjoy themselves.

Oh, they still had to obey the laws of nature, but they did it with much greater freedom, and I think, joy (if chickens can feel such an emotion).

We, too, have come out from under the terrible weight and confinement of the Law of sin and death—a Law that demanded an impossible perfection. We have come under the rule of a new law. Turn to Romans 3:27-28:

> *"Where is boasting then? It is excluded. By what law? Of works? No, but by the law of faith. Therefore we conclude that a man is justified by faith apart from the deeds of the Law."*

The "Law of Faith!" Now what do you suppose that means? With all kinds of ceremonial requirements, and the nagging obligation of numberless ordinances, the Jews were held in strong control by the Law. Now, through Jesus Christ, they have liberty. But this does not mean that a person can live like the devil. Listen to what the Bible says in James 1:25:

> *"But he who looks into the perfect law of liberty and continues in it, and is not a forgetful hearer but a doer of the word, this one will be blessed in what he does."*

How we live, and what we do is still very important in the eyes of God. God's moral laws have never been abrogated. They still stand. Listen to James 2:11-12:

> *"For He who said, 'Do not commit adultery,' also said, 'Do not murder.' Now if you do not commit adultery, but you do murder, you have become a transgressor of the Law. So speak and so do as those who will be judged by the law of liberty."*

Our motivation for living "righteously" is no longer fear, but love: the love of God, and a love of righteousness which comes from a changed heart. As Jesus said in John 14:15:

> *"If you love Me, keep My commandments."*

The changed heart is a direct result of the changed law. Rather than impose His demands from the exterior demands of the Law, God now brings about our obedience through the simple expedient of our liberty in His love.

We'll still be judged for the works done in the flesh—and that's serious. But more than that, we don't have to try to be saved through our own efforts in obeying all the detailed Laws of God. We are saved through faith. And this applies to everyone: whether they knew and had the Laws of God, or whether they were Gentiles without the written Law. Look at Romans 3:29-31:

> *"Or is He the God of the Jews only? Is He not also the God of the Gentiles? Yes, of the Gentiles also, since there is one God who will justify the circumcised by faith and the uncircumcised through faith. Do we then make void the Law through faith? Certainly not! On the contrary, we establish the Law."*

God's original plan was based on love. Look at Deuteronomy 11:13:

> *"And it shall be that if you earnestly obey My commandments which I command you today, to love the Lord your God and serve Him with all your heart and with all your soul...."*

Love for God was always to be the premise of obedience, and later in Romans 5:5 we read:

> *"...because the love of God has been poured out in our hearts by the Holy Spirit who was given to us."*

Faith makes our relationship with God very personal. This is the law of faith and of liberty!

Work Is For A Salary —
Not Salvation!

Romans 4:1-8

If someone, whom you didn't really know, offered you a $50 bill, what would you think? You'd have a few questions, right? What's he up to? What kind of a trick is this? Nobody goes around offering $50 bills to whomever will take it! There must be some catch. Yet, the possibility of $50 without having to work for it does seem like an attractive offer, doesn't it? Well, a gift is a gift! I'll explain why you should take it.

Some years ago, I was in a meeting where an evangelist took a $50 bill from his pocket, and made quite a production of the fact that this $50 was equal to a full day's salary. As you can guess, this was back when salaries were a bit lower than they are today.

The evangelist went on at great length to explain that if anyone wanted this $50, they would be welcome to work for it all day, starting tomorrow morning. Then he offered an alternative. He said, on the other hand, anyone who wants this $50 can walk right up here now, and take it.

The congregation just sat and stared at him. He reemphasized it. Anyone, anyone at all, come and take this. It's free! You don't have to do anything but come up here and receive it. After quite a long silence and wait, finally a woman stood to her feet, went forward, and was given the $50 bill. She returned to her seat with a look of wonder on her face.

This is as good an illustration of what the Bible teaches in Romans chapter four as I have ever seen. Look first with me at Romans 4:4:

> *"Now to him who works, the wages are not counted as grace but as debt."*

After a week of work, my employer owes me a week's salary. It's mine by right. I worked for it, deserve it, and it's mine. There is no mercy, grace or special kindness on the part of my employer in giving me what I earned. Work is for a salary, or wages. But God's favour is not earned. Salvation is not something we can receive as a debt that is due to us. Salvation is like receiving that unearned $50 bill. Look at Romans 4:5:

> *"But to him who does not work but believes on Him who justifies the ungodly, his faith is accounted for righteousness...."*

Just by believing, we receive God's salvation offered through Jesus Christ. Now read with me from Romans 4:1-3:

> *"What then shall we say that Abraham our father has found according to the flesh? For if Abraham was justified by works, he has something to boast about, but not before God. For what does the Scripture say? 'Abraham believed God, and it was accounted to him for righteousness'" (Genesis 15:6).*

Many people seem to be under the impression that they must somehow please God before they can claim His free offer of salvation. They perhaps feel they must push the average of good actions up over 50% as opposed to bad actions. Or perhaps, if they make some special sacrifice of some kind, they can curry God's favour. Perhaps you are caught up in some method of trying to please God, and thus "buy" His favour. Yet we just read of Abraham, whom the Bible calls the "Father of the Faithful," that he simply "believed" God, and it was accounted as righteousness.

Now this is not to say that good actions, good works, and obedience to God are not important. They are! But the starting point with God is not works, but faith. "Without faith it is impossible to please God" (Hebrews 11:6).

Paul refers back again to the Old Testament, and King David, who wrote Psalm 32. Let's read that quote from Romans 4:7-8:

> *"Blessed are those whose lawless deeds are forgiven, and whose sins are covered; blessed is the man to whom the Lord shall not impute sin."*

Christians are not perfect. They're just forgiven. Christians are people who have accepted God's offer of free salvation, aside from works. Faith has simply reached out and received the $50 bill, even though there was really no reason to deserve it.

But one thing many Christians need to know is that once they have accepted this free salvation, they also have an obligation to live the lifestyle of a true Christian, with a full understanding that the moral Laws of God still define sin and righteousness.

The law of faith was in effect, long before the Laws of Moses, as we will see in our next study.

A Lesson In Accounting

Romans 4:9-15

I suppose we all have bank accounts. Some are empty, some are full, and some are overdrawn. I like to keep accounts to try to avoid being overdrawn, and also to know precisely how much I have in my account. But how do you handle your accounts when suddenly your account is full, and you did nothing at all to make it full? I work for what I earn, but I had a real surprise in my account one day, something I couldn't account for. I thought...well...read on and I'll tell you what I thought!

Some long years ago I had a rather startling experience with my bank. It was in the days before banking machines. In fact, it was in the days when you had to go to the teller for everything. It was wonderful, at least for a little while.

I was updating my bank book. I found a balance of over $10,000 in my account. I stared at it, and wondered who the kind person was who had made a direct deposit into my personal account to the tune of $10,000. When I asked if there was any way I could find out who had put this into my account, they began to search their records. A few minutes later, the teller came to me with a very red face, and said she was very sorry, but an error had been made in a business account deposit, and they had mistakenly credited me with $10,000. Well, it felt good for a few minutes. But when I thought of it later, I was happy I had not spent any of it. I could have built up a pretty massive debt!

There is a similarity here with the deposit of righteousness that God puts into our account, in response to our faith, not our actions, and regardless of ethnic connections. Look first at Romans 4:9:

> *"Does this blessedness then come upon the circumcised only, or upon the uncircumcised also? For we say that faith was accounted to Abraham for righteousness. How then was it accounted? While he was circumcised, or uncircumcised? Not while circumcised, but while uncircumcised."*

Even before the Law which both defined and demanded righteousness was given by God, Abraham had a deposit of righteousness in his account, by simply believing God. Before circumcision, before the legal ceremonies given through Moses, before any of the Law was in effect, faith filled Abraham's account. We see in Romans 4:12b-13 that it was not for just the Jews. Let's read it:

> *"...God is Father...not only (of those who) are of the circumcision, but (those) who also walk in the steps of the faith which our father Abraham had while still uncircumcised. For the promise that he would be the heir of the world was not to Abraham or to his seed through the Law, but through the righteousness of faith."*

God reckons people who simply believe Him and are willing to do His will as righteous! No prerequisites, no conditions to be met in advance, just faith—simple believing! Paul mentions Abraham's faith a little later in chapter four of Romans. Read Romans 4:21-22 with me:

> *"...and (Abraham) being fully convinced that what He (God) had promised He was also able to perform. And therefore it was accounted to him for righteousness."*

Just like that undeserved and unearned $10,000 which had been put in my account, Abraham's faith was "accounted" to him for righteousness. Now, the $10,000 that was put into my account at the bank was a mistake. But the righteousness which God imputes to your account because of faith is no mistake! It is His ultimate plan and purpose that you have an account full of righteousness.

Now where do you suppose this account is held? Could it possibly be the heart of man...that inner core of your being which, before God's righteousness filled it, was filled with something else? Look back to Romans 2:5:

> *"But in accordance with your hardness and your impenitent heart you are treasuring up for yourself wrath in the day of wrath and revelation of the righteous judgment of God...."*

Now listen to what Jesus said, in Matthew 5:20:

> *"For I say to you, that unless your righteousness exceeds the righteousness of the scribes and Pharisees, you will by no means enter the Kingdom of Heaven."*

You see, the righteousness which counts with God, starts with God. He credits it to our account when we simply believe Him, unlike the Pharisees who just made a show of it while their hearts were far from God. And when we face the righteous judgment of God, and give account of ourselves, it won't be on the basis of our own righteousnesses which are filthy rags, but on the righteousness which He alone can give.

Have You Ever Met Grace?

Romans 4:16-18

Have you ever been driving just above the speed limit, and suddenly you see a police car? Your foot just automatically comes off the accelerator, and you begin coasting, slowing down slightly. I have. And I glance at the speedometer and realize I'm still going too fast. My first thought is, "I've had it! And I deserve it!" But then, as you keep glancing in the rear view mirror, you see the police car sitting still—no flashing lights—he's not after you! Do you know why? Maybe it was because "Grace" was in the police car too!

Very few people I know are perfectly good! Any one of us, if we are honest even for just a few seconds, would claim to never ever have stolen anything. Even if it was just a pencil, or an eraser when we were just kids in primary school, I dare say none of us is perfect when it comes to stealing. Or perhaps, just in the last few months on the income tax return? And that's just in the area of stealing. What about other areas, like, telling the truth; the unshaded truth at all times? How about what many consider the more serious stuff, like, murder, adultery or gossip? Paul asked the question, in Romans 2:21:

> *"You who preach that a man should not steal, do you steal?"*

He makes a good point! Even the preacher is human, and weak. Being good is difficult. Acting good is not too difficult, but being good is really not quite the same. So, if you've been honest with me in these last 30 seconds or so, we have a problem. Most of the wrongs we've done in life cannot be made right. Oh some can, and both you and I have likely gone to someone we have wronged, asked for forgiveness, and have settled the matter. But there are probably a whole string of wrongs that now are impossible to make right. In other words, if I got what I deserved, I'd be dead meat!

Now, we've been talking about being righteous. Walking a "strait" path. Being good, if you like. So, with all these unsettled and unsettling wrongs in our personal histories, how can we become good, and wipe the slate clean?

Well, let me introduce you to grace. Grace was a fact, long before it was a girl's name. Grace is the favour of God, unearned, and undeserved. That's why we cannot get God's favour, forgiveness and salvation by the things we do. It is not by works, but by simply believing. Look at Romans 4:16-17:

> *"Therefore it is of faith that it might be according to grace...."*

If it was not undeserved, and unearned, it would be a debt. But God does not accept our efforts at being good enough, whether we had the Law or didn't have the Law to guide us.

> "...so that the promise might be sure to all the seed, not only to those who are of the Law, but also to those who are of the faith of Abraham, who is the father of us all (as it is written, 'I have made you a father of many nations') in the presence of Him whom he believed...."

The father of many nations. Not just the father of the Jews and the Arabs, but the father of all the Gentile nations as well, who had the faith to receive God's provision, without the works of the Law. Abraham believed God when He promised him a son even in his (and Sarah's) old age. When the possibility of children was long past, he simply believed God could do what God said He would do. We read on:

> "...God, who gives life to the dead and calls those things which do not exist as though they did...."

So Abraham believed God. Even in the face of the fact that he had no son through whom the promise could be fulfilled, and Sarah's womb (at age 90) was effectively dead. But, because God said it, Abraham believed it even in the face of no hope. Look at Romans 4:18:

> "...who, contrary to hope, in hope believed, so that he became the father of many nations, according to what was spoken, 'So shall your descendants be.'"

Paul makes it clear to us, that faith was more important to God than the fulfilling of the Law, because before the Law existed, God honoured faith. And because this is so, we can all appeal to the grace of God; that undeserved and unearned favour of God, without having to have recourse to the Law. Later Paul writes to Christians, in Ephesians 2:8:

> "For by grace you have been saved through faith, and that not of yourselves; it is the gift of God."

Today we've met "Grace." In our next study we'll meet "Faith."

Have You Ever Met Faith?

Romans 4:19-25

I don't suppose it is possible to get a full understanding of faith, in just two pages of commentary. But I'm going to try. We hear so many things being said about faith, that a lot of folk are confused. The answer to this confusion is in the Bible. It's not only the source of faith itself, but it's the source of our understanding of what faith really is. I know that a few minutes can't solve all the confusion, but it can help.

What is faith? We do hear a great deal about faith in Christian circles these days, and some even advertise it as though they have an exclusive on it. Is there any place in the Bible which really defines what faith is? As a matter of fact, there is! Look at Hebrews 11:1:

> *"Now faith is the substance of things hoped for, the evidence of things not seen."*

Faith accepts as an accomplished fact, that when God makes a promise, it's as good as done. No questions, no hesitation. If God says it will happen, then it's as good as done. That's precisely what Paul was describing in the experience of Abraham, in Romans 4:19-21:

> *"And not being weak in faith, he (Abraham) did not consider his own body, already dead (since he was about 100 years old), and the dead-ness of Sarah's womb. He did not waver at the promise of God through unbelief, but was strengthened in faith, giving glory to God, and being fully convinced that what He had promised He was also able to perform."*

There is the crux of the whole matter of faith: "...being fully convinced that what He (God) had promised, He is also able to perform." Christian faith is rooted in God Himself. It is belief that God is both righteous and faithful in His promise, and He is powerful enough to actually make it happen, even in the face of impossible odds. True faith is rooted in God. It is not rooted in our own desires, no matter how desperate they may be. It is not rooted in a method of prayer. Faith cannot be confined to a definition, or a formula. It is founded in, and comes from God. Abraham had that simple faith. And as we read in Romans 4:22-25:

> *"And therefore it was accounted to him for righteousness."*

Abraham was designated "righteous" by God, simply because He took God's Word to him at face value. But it doesn't stop with Abraham. Look at the rest of these few verses:

> *"Now it was not written for his sake alone that it was imputed to him, but also for us. It (righteousness) shall be imputed to us who believe in Him who raised up Jesus our Lord from the dead, who was delivered up because of our offenses, and was raised because of our justification."*

Well, you may say, "There's a difference. God was actually talking to Abraham. God has never talked to me!"

I beg your pardon! That's what this book is all about! The Bible is God talking to you, through its history, through its teaching, through its Saviour, Jesus Christ. Look at Hebrews 1:1-2:

> *"God, who at various times and in various ways spoke in time past to the fathers by the prophets, has in these last days spoken to us by His Son, whom He has appointed Heir of all things, through whom also He made the worlds."*

If you're not hearing God speak to you, you're not listening. The Bible is God's voice; God's design for life and godliness; God's truth. If you're not hearing, it's because you're not listening. And when you do listen, and hear the voice of God through His Word, and through the Christ of the Word, you, too, will have faith. Here is what is written a little later, in Romans 10:17:

> *"So then faith comes by hearing, and hearing by the Word of God."*

Faith doesn't come by listening to any specific preacher, or going to any specific church. Faith is not rooted in those things, as good and as faithful as they may be to God's Word. Faith is rooted in the very character of God Himself.

Do be careful about people who claim greater faith than others. Paul warns us in Romans 12:3:

> *"For I say, through the grace given to me, to everyone who is among you, not to think of himself more highly than he ought to think, but to think soberly, as God has dealt to each one a measure of faith."*

That's why I believe you have enough faith to approach God for yourself. You, too, have a measure of faith! At least enough to get started toward God!

Getting Back Together Again
Romans 5:1-11

Have you ever been so offended by someone that you simply avoided their company? Sometimes even the best of friends break off all relationships when one of them offends the other. And the longer it lasts, the worse it gets. Even though there are regrets, the original offense was such a great offense, such a sin, that reconciliation is impossible. Well, there is a way! Yes, there is a way of getting back together again!

I'm sure we've all heard the stories of the feud between the Hatfields and the McCoys. A feud between families can be a terrible thing. The hate and recriminations go on and on for generations. The McCoy children are raised and taught to hate the Hatfields, and the Hatfields teach their children to hate the McCoys and to take every opportunity to hurt them. The offended ones, on both sides of the feud, sit and brood for hours over the injustices and hatefulness of the other. For generations it goes on, and any thoughts of peace between them, much less reconciliation, are dismissed with a growl...until the favourite son of the McCoys falls in love with the favourite daughter of the Hatfields.

Although it's an inadequate illustration, it does picture the great gulf between God and man, ever since God was offended by man's sin.

Yet God sent His beloved Son, Jesus Christ, into the middle of the enemy camp, to get a bride. And He was willing to cancel all the sin, hate and offense of the past and to accept sinners as though they had never sinned. That's what the Bible means when it talks about being justified. Look at Romans 5:1-2:

> *"Therefore, having been justified by faith, we have peace with God through our Lord Jesus Christ, through whom also we have access by faith into this grace in which we stand, and rejoice in hope of the glory of God."*

The separation between God and man was massive in its proportions. And to make it worse, the way man chose to live, away from God's design, away from God's straight path, caused man to weaken and die. Living in a way other than the way God planned has that effect! God doesn't kill men off. God wants fellowship with men. It is "evil" that kills men off. Look at Psalms 34:21:

> *"Evil shall slay the wicked, and those who hate the righteous shall be condemned."*

So mankind, progressively weakened by sin, unrighteousness and evil, becomes helpless: literally unable to help itself. Then God steps in and we read in Romans 5:6:

> *"For when we were still without strength, in due time Christ died for the ungodly."*

And the amazing motive for this is love? A totally committed, unconditional love. John 3:16 says it best:

> *"For God so loved the world, that He gave His only Son...."*

God wanted the feud over. He wanted fellowship between man and Himself. He wanted peace, but not just peace. He wanted reconciliation. That means a closeness in fellowship and association. And He was prepared to more than talk about it. He would take action, and demonstrate that love. Look at Romans 5:8-11:

> *"But God demonstrates His own love toward us, in that while we were still sinners, Christ died for us. Much more then, having now been justified by His blood, we shall be saved from wrath through Him. For if when we were enemies we were reconciled to God through the death of His Son, much more, having been reconciled, we shall be saved by His life. And not only that, but we also rejoice in God through our Lord Jesus Christ, through whom we have now received the reconciliation."*

That makes me pretty grateful to Jesus Christ. He provided the way, the only way I could get back to God. And more than that, He keeps me in that way after I have been reconciled with God. "Having been reconciled, we shall be saved by His life." Jesus Christ lives! He lives in me! And His life provides not only access to God's righteousness, but the ability and strength to live righteously. Even though I have no inheritance from the Jews or from the Law, I, a Gentile, can know God personally. Look at Colossians 1:27:

> *"God willed to make known what are the riches of the glory of this mystery among the Gentiles: which is Christ in you, the Hope of glory."*

Have you any room at all for Jesus Christ in your life? I assure you, that a ful-filled life is impossible without this reconciliation with God!

Act And Counteract

Romans 5:12-21

Wouldn't it be great to start off life retired? All the food, entertainment and services you could ever wish for, paid in advance, and you could live the life of Riley right from the beginning. No blood, sweat and tears to provide for yourself; not even any pain or sickness—guaranteed? I know of one man who had that privilege. It wasn't even inherited from his parents. But he blew it! Let me tell you about this chap called Adam.

It all started when Adam got off track. A perfect life had been designed for Adam and his wife. A very simple set of rules, within which Adam should live, was set in place. Everything was laid on! Food, fellowship with God, recreation, entertainment, perfect health, and life forever. Not a ripple on the silver platter of life's joy. Everything was perfect, everything was just right— total righteousness prevailed. Until Adam's failure.

Adam, knowing the few restrictions that God had imposed, chose to disobey. His disobedience became what is known as the "principle of sin." That is the innate bent toward wrong which pervades every soul from Adam to you. Adam was responsible for the sin principle which passes onto all men everywhere. You and I are responsible for the individual acts of sin of which every one of us is guilty. These are the outworking of that sin principle with which we are all born. Here's what we are told in Romans 5:12-14:

> *"Therefore, just as through one man sin entered the world, and death through sin, and thus death spread to all men, because all sinned— (For until the Law sin was in the world, but sin is not imputed when there is no law. Nevertheless death reigned from Adam to Moses, even over those who had not sinned according to the likeness of the transgression of Adam, who is a type of Him who was to come...).*"

That first "act" of sin by Adam was an offense to God. But Jesus, Who is sometimes known as the "Second Adam," came and lived a perfect life. Now these two were in totally different leagues. Adam was created man. Jesus was God come in the likeness of man. Adam sinned. Jesus did not sin. And Jesus, though sinless in life, took upon Himself the sins and offenses of all men everywhere. He died for our sins. And in exchange for those many offenses of man, He offers justification, freely, by His grace. We read in Romans 5:15-16:

> *"But the free gift is not like the offense. For if by the one man's offense many died, much more the grace of God and the gift by the grace of the one Man, Jesus Christ, abounded to many. And the gift is*

*not like that which came through the one who sinned. For the judg-
ment which came from one offense resulted in condemnation, but the
free gift which came from many offenses resulted in justification."*

I'm reminded of a little chorus I learned some years ago, which highlights that truth:

"He paid a debt He did not owe,
I owed a debt I could not pay,
I needed Someone, to wash my sins away,
And now I sing a brand new song: Amazing Grace,
Christ Jesus paid a debt that I could never pay!"

You see, when Adam sinned, he brought down the whole weight of the Law on himself, and the whole human race. Romans 6:23 says:

"The wages of sin is death...."

Falling short of God's standards for mankind is a punishable offense. And you and I have continued in the tradition of Adam, in disobedience. But Jesus came, in the likeness and yes, weakness, of human flesh, yet obeyed God in every thought and action. Thus we read in Romans 5:19:

*"For as by one man's disobedience many were made sinners, so also
by one Man's obedience many will be made righteous."*

We cannot assume though, that just like every man was affected by Adam's sin, so we are all affected by Jesus' sinlessness, as though it is automatic. Look at Acts 13:38-39:

*"Therefore let it be known to you, brethren, that through this Man is
preached to you the forgiveness of sins; and by Him everyone who
believes is justified from all things from which you could not be justified by the Law of Moses."*

The key is faith—just believing. Jesus said in John 3:36:

*"He who believes in the Son has everlasting life; and he who does
not believe the Son shall not see life, but the wrath of God abides on
him."*

You don't have to be a nuclear physicist to understand that!

Dead Men Don't Sin
Romans 6:1-14

I really feel sorry for men and women who are doctors. They are on the front lines in the fight against sickness, disease, and physical disabilities. And yet they know better than any, that no matter how long they are able to delay death, in the end, death comes. And death is the only cure for some diseases. It's the same in the matter of sin. Death is the only real, final cure for sin. And, I guess that's what the Apostle Paul meant when he said we should all reckon ourselves as dead meat!

The story is told of a very famous bank robber out in the west at the turn of the century. In the process of robbing banks, he had also killed several people. He had been caught, went through a rather quick trial, and was sentenced to death by hanging. After the sentence had been carried out, two townsmen, standing and watching the dead body swinging in the tree had a few terse comments. The first man said, "Well, there's your murdering thief!" The second man said, "He's no murdering thief any more, he's just plain dead!"

In other words, "Dead men don't sin!" After what we have learned about the grace of God and how we don't have to earn that grace by obeying the Law, Paul premeditates what some might say. Look at Romans 6:1-3:

> *"What shall we say then? Shall we continue in sin that grace may abound? Certainly not! How shall we who died to sin live any longer in it? Or do you not know that as many of us as were baptized into Christ Jesus were baptized into His death?"*

In other words, Paul says, there's more to it than just receiving God's salvation through faith. This same faith identifies us with the death of Christ. We died with Him by faith. And dead men don't sin. That accounts for the remarkable difference in people's lives when they become believing Christians. Romans 6:4-7 says:

> *"Therefore we were buried with Him through baptism into death, that just as Christ was raised from the dead by the glory of the Father, even so we also should walk in newness of life. For if we have been united together in the likeness of His death, certainly we also shall be in the likeness of His resurrection, knowing this, that our old man was crucified with Him, that the body of sin might be done away with, that we should no longer be slaves of sin. For he who has died has been freed from sin."*

There, the Bible says it. Dead men don't sin! And it makes no difference to God whether you are a Jew under the Law, or a Gentile with only a conscience. Look at what the Bible says in Galatians 6:15:

"For in Christ Jesus neither circumcision (Jews) nor uncircumcision (Gentiles) avails anything, but a new creation."

We become new people, born again, redeemed from the powers of darkness when we identify with Jesus Christ through faith in His death and resurrection. Again, the Bible says in 2 Corinthians 5:17:

"Therefore, if anyone is in Christ, he is a new creation; old things have passed away; behold, all things have become new."

This new life that comes to the believing Christian is the life of Christ, including the "life-style" of Jesus Christ. Oh yes, as long as we are in these mortal bodies there will be temptations to return to the old life-style of sin, dishonesty, lust, and unrighteousness. As long as mortal life continues, there will be the temptation to step off the "strait" path and take our own way that could again lead to destruction. But we are told we have a choice now. Look at Romans 6:12-13:

"Therefore do not let sin reign in your mortal body, that you should obey it in its lusts. And do not present your members as instruments of unrighteousness to sin, but present yourselves to God as being alive from the dead, and your members as instruments of righteousness to God."

Present yourself to God, on a daily basis. His life within you will provide the strength to resist sin, and to resist temptation. God can guide you through the minefield of this sinful world. Look at the assurance of that, given by God in 1 Corinthians 10:13:

"No temptation has overtaken you except such as is common to man; but God is faithful, who will not allow you to be tempted beyond what you are able, but with the temptation will also make the way of escape, that you may be able to bear it."

Dead men don't sin. As a Christian, reckon yourself to be dead to sin, then live that way!

Slavery Is Not All Bad

Romans 6:15-23

At what point is a person considered an habitual criminal? Our local newspaper reported a young man who had been put into jail on five different occasions for the same offense. Do you suppose he has actually come to like jail? Or is it because he has become slave to a lifestyle that just happens to be an offense to the laws of Canada? Whatever the case, he's a slave, either to his habits or to his jailers. There must be a better form of slavery than that! In fact, I know a form of slavery that I actually recommend!

My wife read a report to me from the local newspaper. It was about a young man who had just gone to court for a criminal offense. The remarkable aspect of this report is that it was the fifth time he had been convicted of a crime that he just kept on committing.

He had been in jail before. But he had been set free, after paying his debt to society with six months in prison. I don't know whether or not it was explained to him, when he was released the last time, that he was free! He had no debt to society now. He had paid in full, and now he was no longer under the power of the law in prison. Yet, as soon as he was out of jail, he discovered he was not really free. He was slave to actions and a way of life that was contrary to the law. It seemed he was always in a prison; either in jail, or in the style of life that had him bound up as surely as any jail.

When the price is paid to society, the hope is that the offender will change his habits. It's much the same when we, who are all offenders of the Laws of God, have been given our freedom through God's grace. The idea is to stay away from the things that offend the Law. Look at Romans 6:15-16:

> *"What then? Shall we sin because we are not under Law but under grace? Certainly not! Do you not know that to whom you present yourselves slaves to obey, you are that one's slaves whom you obey, whether of sin leading to death, or of obedience leading to righteousness?"*

Slavery is inevitable. Either you are a slave of sin, bound and controlled, or you are a willing slave of God, with almost limitless freedom. So slavery isn't all bad. If you are a slave of God, you will enjoy greater freedom and joy than you could ever have repeating the behaviour that brings you back into the bondage of the devil. Look now at Romans 6:18-19:

"And having been set free from sin, you became slaves of righteousness. I speak in human terms because of the weakness of your flesh. For just as you presented your members as slaves of uncleanness, and of lawlessness leading to more lawlessness, so now present your members as slaves of righteousness for holiness."

It is no sin to be tempted toward evil and unrighteousness. The devil makes it his business to try to trip people into sin. The sin is not in the temptation, but in the doing. And now, living as a child of God, and as a willing slave to His righteousness, you have eternal life in view. It is not that this new good behaviour earns you eternal life. Rather, this is a gift from God, already provided by Jesus having paid the debt. You are now free. You don't have to go back into jail again. Romans 6:22-23 says:

"But now having been set free from sin, and having become slaves of God, you have your fruit to holiness, and the end, everlasting life. For the wages of sin is death, but the gift of God is eternal life in Christ Jesus our Lord."

That young man reported in the newspaper obviously chose to abuse the freedom he had regained, several times. And he's not that different from many who call themselves Christians, and abuse the new-found freedom they have found in Jesus Christ. It is possible for Christians to find themselves back in the grip of sin. That's why the Bible says, in 2 Peter 2:20:

"For if, after they have escaped the pollutions of the world through the knowledge of the Lord and Saviour Jesus Christ, they are again entangled in them and overcome, the latter end is worse for them than the beginning."

After five offenses against the law, that young criminal got a much more severe sentence than previously.

The point is, if you live right, you don't have to worry about the law!

Dead Men Don't Go To Jail

Romans 7:1-6

I'm not a lawyer, but I do know this about the law. It has to be obeyed! I also know that the law was designed for our good, even though I question some of the new laws being imposed on our society in recent years. Another thing I know about the law is that there are some people who are above the law. Perhaps a better term would be below the law. These people to whom the law does not apply are dead. And that's why the law can't touch them. You can't put a dead man in jail!

There have been cases throughout history, and throughout the world, where courts have passed sentence on a criminal who has fled the country. If that person were ever to return, that sentence would be imposed. But if he dies, that's the end of the case. It doesn't do much good to send a dead man to jail. And if someone does die while he's in jail, there is certainly no thought of keeping him in jail until the whole sentence is served. The law has little power over a dead man. With that in mind, look at Romans 7:1:

> *"Or do you not know, brethren (for I speak to those who know the Law [the Jews]), that the Law has dominion over a man as long as he lives?"*

The idea that we can earn forgiveness, and God's favour, by obeying a list of rules and regulations has to be put to death. We gain our salvation by simply believing in Jesus Christ. Obeying rules, such as the constitution and by-laws of a denomination, may get you membership in one of their churches, but that doesn't wash with God. The only thing that washes, with God, is the blood of the Lord Jesus Christ. By shedding His blood for the sins of the world, He opens up the way to God and by-passes all the Laws and Ordinances.

Now I used one illustration but we find a better one in Romans 7:2-3:

> *"For the woman who has a husband is bound by the law to her husband as long as he lives. But if the husband dies, she is released from the law of her husband. So then if, while her husband lives, she marries another man, she will be called an adulteress; but if her husband dies, she is free from that law, so that she is no adulteress, though she has married another man."*

Death brings an end to the domination of the Law over us. When we accept the work of Jesus Christ on Calvary, we die to the Law. We enter into the likeness of the death of Jesus Christ, and are freed from the passions and control of sin as defined by the Law. Occasionally we will find those same passions thrown up into our faces, but we don't have to obey those passions any longer. We obey the new law of faith and righteousness. Look at Romans 7:5-6:

> *"For when we were in the flesh, the sinful passions which were aroused by the Law were at work in our members to bear fruit to death. But now we have been delivered from the Law, having died to what we were held by, so that we should serve in the newness of the Spirit and not in the oldness of the letter."*

This new freedom and life in the Spirit is not a license to sin. It's a clear recognition that we were unable to attain righteousness from our own resources, and that only God's provision through Jesus Christ is sufficient. This is made clear in 2 Corinthians 3:5-6:

> *"Not that we are sufficient of ourselves to think of anything as being from ourselves, but our sufficiency is from God, who also made us sufficient as ministers of the new covenant, not of the letter but of the Spirit; for the letter kills, but the Spirit gives life."*

As a Canadian people, we take pride in the fact that we believe in the rule of law. We take pride in the fact that these laws are designed to protect the law-abiding citizen against the lawbreakers. And when someone does break the law, it provides for a severe decrease in freedom. The worse the crime, the harsher the sentence. This applies to everyone in Canada, citizen or visitor, Christian or heathen. We must all obey the laws.

But for the Christian, we have been delivered both from the rule of the religious laws and from the punishment of the law, to the greater freedom found through faith in Jesus Christ.

You can't punish a dead man, and we have died to the law!

Don't Touch That!

Romans 7:7-12

Did you ever tell your child, "Don't touch that stove! It's hot! It'll burn you!" Then of course the crying and running to father with a burnt finger seemed almost inevitable. Why? My saying it would burn wasn't what made it burn. The stove was already dangerous! My warning just focused his attention, and made it attractive to his rebellious little nature. Should I have not told him? And just hoped that he'd blunder safely through life?

My wife and I have raised two children. They were wonderful children when they were little, and I'm of the opinion that they are pretty good adults. Now, raising children, as any of you who have had the joy know, is not without its problems. There is something in the nature of all of us that begins to show very early in life. It's rebellion.

Sometimes it's better to not even mention that some things are wrong to do, because the very mentioning of them stirs up that little rebellious nature. From that moment on, there is a nagging desire for the child to do exactly the thing he was warned against. Have you ever had that experience? You tell a child not to touch a hot stove, and suddenly from that moment, the child hovers around the stove, wondering what will happen if he does touch it. When he gets close, you reinforce the rule, "Don't touch that! It'll hurt you!"

Now the strange thing is this. To touch the stove was wrong, even before you mentioned it. But now that you've mentioned it, he knows it's wrong, but now by his very nature, he's attracted toward that wrong. Does this sound familiar? Doesn't this very same nature live in you and I, even though we may have become a bit more sophisticated in our expression of it? Read with me in Romans 7:7-8:

> *"What shall we say then? Is the Law sin? Certainly not! On the contrary, I would not have known sin except through the Law. For I would not have known covetousness unless the Law had said, "You shall not covet." But sin, taking opportunity by the commandment, produced in me all manner of evil desire. For apart from the Law sin was dead."*

If I had never told my son that to touch the stove was wrong, he would never have known. But that would not have made a scrap of difference if he had touched the stove. He'd still have been burned! So I had to warn him, and give him at least the opportunity to avoid disaster. Now look at Romans 7:9-10:

"I was alive once without the Law, but when the commandment came, sin revived and I died. And the commandment, which was to bring life, I found to bring death."

The warnings of the Law are for us to avoid disaster! God's Laws and rules are not to keep us from having fun in life, they are to help us live a happy and protected life. It's not the Law that kills us, it's the breaking of the Law that brings death. Our very nature is suddenly and clearly revealed to every one of us as soon as we are confronted with a list of rules. We want to break the rules, just to assert our own identity! And that, when it is boiled down to its very essence, is simply pride! And that's the stuff that comes just prior to destruction!

So, the Laws of God show me what sin is and what sin does to me. They're a warning against disaster. "Don't touch that stove, it'll burn you!" But our own rebellious human nature, rising up against the rules of God, deceives me into thinking I can get away with it! But sin kills me. Look at Romans 7:11-12:

"For sin, taking occasion by the commandment, deceived me, and by it killed me. Therefore the Law is holy, and the commandment holy and just and good."

So the Law is good, and right. Its purpose is to keep me from disaster, and even though I may not fully understand why it is wrong to do certain things, I must at least recognize that in God's plan for man, there is a blueprint for success, and that deviations from that blueprint are inviting problems. But just how serious a deviation really is, is known only through God's clearly revealed Word.

The Law therefore, is like a school teacher, acquainting us with the facts about what is good for us, and what is bad for us. And as it turns out, breaking God's rules is sin, and that is extremely bad for us!

The Nature Of The Beast

Romans 7:13-26

Trying to teach a hunting hound to forsake his basic nature and become a house pet is a very difficult, if not impossible, job. Their noses are built for tracking, their stamina is for running down their prey. It's the very nature of the beast to get on a trail and hunt. Trying to change that nature is like sewing buttons on jello. It just won't last. The best we can hope for is a bit of control. Does this sound theological to you?

We have two dogs with a high proportion of "hound" in them. They love the out-of-doors, and we just don't dare let the both of them outside, untied, at the same time. If they do get out together, they're gone. For at least a half a day, we won't see them. They're off into the bush and along the river, chasing everything from rabbits to fox or even deer, I suppose.

You see, these two dogs are natural hunters. It's in their very nature to take up the chase. They'll chase live animals, and if they come across something that isn't alive, they'll roll around on their backs on their decomposing discoveries. They are hunters—it's the nature of the beast! It's so deeply ingrained in them, it will never be eradicated as long as they live.

Actually, I'm not that much different myself! There's something in my nature that is so deeply ingrained that as long as I live, I'll be fighting it! And, lest you start to get a bit smug, let me warn you: you're not much different from me in this respect. The Bible calls it our carnal nature. Look at Romans 7:14-15:

> *"For we know that the Law is spiritual, but I am carnal, sold under sin. For what I am doing, I do not understand. For what I will to do, that I do not practice; but what I hate, that I do."*

Every one of us has had this disconcerting experience. We find ourselves doing something wrong, even while at the same time our conscience keeps yelling at us to do right! It applies in a thousand ways in our lives. We know something is wrong, and we do it anyway. But the very fact that we know it is wrong betrays to us that we recognize that there have to be rules. Let us read on in Romans 7:16-17 now:

> *"If, then, I do what I will not to do, I agree with the Law that it is good. But now, it is no longer I who do it, but sin that dwells in me."*

So we find that, in spite of our desire to do what is right, there appears to be something in our very nature that overpowers right. The Bible calls this sin. And this principle of sin is in the very nature of the beast—in every single one of us—without exception. In our own mind, we prefer to do the right thing. Even though no one told us not to touch the hot stove, we know it's wrong, and that the consequences are terrible. But we still flit around the hot stove until we're burned. Paul the Apostle says the same thing in Romans 7:22-23:

> *"For I delight in the Law of God according to the inward man. But I see another law in my members, warring against the law of my mind, and bringing me into captivity to the law of sin which is in my members."*

Just as my beautiful dogs have this deeply-embedded love of hunting, we have the deeply-embedded love of sinning. It's the nature of the beast with the dog. With man, you and me, it's a part of our fallen nature. And there's nothing we can do about it! No amount of surgery or social reform can take it out of us. No determination of mind can bring about a perfect performance. Sin is too deeply embedded in our carnal nature. As long as we are in this human body, we've got to live with that fact!

Yet God still wants us to be perfect. How in the world can this ever happen? Well, Paul asks the same question in Romans 7:24-25, and gives the answer too. Read with me:

> *"O wretched man that I am! Who will deliver me from this body of death? I thank God—through Jesus Christ our Lord! So then, with the mind I myself serve the Law of God, but with the flesh the law of sin."*

My soul is God's, but my flesh is the world's. In our next study we'll see why Jesus Christ is the answer to this dilemma.

Death Row

Romans 8:1-8

I can't imagine what must have gone through the minds of the Bahutu of Rwanda, when they saw the oncoming Watutsi with guns and spears just minutes before they died. Thousands of them, condemned, just because of the tribe in which they were born. And then the UN troops turned up. The only thing I can compare it to is the horror of the realization of sin's consequence. Yet just in time, Jesus comes on the scene to save us. Death's row is no joke!

I have never had the sad duty of visiting a condemned criminal on death row. But I have read a few accounts by clergy who have had that terrible responsibility. Death row is that series of cells in a high security prison, where those who have been condemned to death await their final farewell to life. It is not a place of hope.

There is little cause for optimism. In fact, the only single hope that some of those who stand condemned have, is that through some final desperate move and some friends, the death sentence might be commuted. Death row is the final horror. Now-a-days, with the death sentence not practiced in Canada, criminals are sentenced to "life" in prison, if you can call that life. In either case, they have been condemned, either to death (in some other countries) or to prison life.

And yet, in a very real sense, that's where you and I have ended up because of sin: Death Row! Because of sin! But, as Paul pointed out in our last study, there is a way out of this condemnation, and Paul says it is through Jesus Christ. Now look at Romans 8:1-2:

> *"There is therefore now no condemnation to those who are in Christ Jesus, who do not walk according to the flesh, but according to the Spirit. For the law of the Spirit of life in Christ Jesus has made me free from the law of sin and death."*

Jesus Christ has delivered us out from under the curse and condemnation of sin. By simply admitting to God that we are sinners, and asking for His mercy and forgiveness, we can have the eternity part of our death sentence commuted. Do you remember what we read back in Romans 5:8?

> *"But God demonstrates His own love toward us, in that while we were still sinners, Christ died for us."*

While we were still on death row (the earned reward of sinning), Jesus died FOR us, taking our criminal rebellion on Himself. He did what even our obedience to law could not have done. Look at Romans 8:3-4:

"For what the Law could not do in that it was weak through the flesh, God did by sending His own Son in the likeness of sinful flesh, on account of sin: He condemned sin in the flesh, that the righteous requirement of the Law might be fulfilled in us who do not walk according to the flesh but according to the Spirit."

No wonder Paul said, "Thank God we can be delivered from this body of death through Jesus Christ!"

But it does take our cooperation. We cannot stand by and say, "Good for God, He looked after my sin." We must agree with God, first of all, that we are indeed sinners, and that there's nothing we can do about it. Then we must accept what Jesus Christ has done for us, but on a very personal basis. Jesus calls it being "born again." Then, when we accept Jesus Christ into our lives and experiences, we must recognize that God's Spirit lives within us. We then simply live the way the Spirit of God within us instructs. That's called "walking according to the Spirit" in verse five of this chapter.

That even more simply means, living by faith, according to God's Laws which now come from within the heart, the dwelling place of God. To do otherwise is to revert to the dictates of the flesh. That's why Paul says in Romans 8:6:

"For to be carnally minded is death, but to be spiritually minded is life and peace."

Remember what Paul said back in chapter six? You become a slave to whomever you choose to obey. And that is the crux of the matter. You do have a choice. But the choice is crucial. Look at Romans 8:8:

"So then, those who are in the flesh cannot please God."

We have already found that without faith we cannot please God. Now we find that, by walking under the guidance and direction of the Holy Spirit, we can please God. Next, we'll learn a bit more about what it means to walk in the Spirit.

The Unweird Way To Live

Romans 8:9-14

Why is it that a person who totally gives himself over to God is called a religious fanatic, and weird? Yet a person who is totally preoccupied with some sport is simply a fan; not weird at all? I want to talk about weird people today, and if that gives you a weird feeling, I suggest you read on. This commentary, I promise you, will not be weird!

Some people are weird! In fact, I think most people on the face of the earth are a little weird. And, after I looked up the term "weird" in the dictionary, I was totally convinced! Do you know what the dictionary meaning of "weird" really is? Here it is:

> *"Concerned with the unnatural, or with witchcraft." (Funk & Wagnalls)*

Weird means... "unnatural"; that which is not normal.

Now, strange as it may seem, the word "weird" has been twisted to even apply to religious mystics and pious people. "That guy's weird, man. He doesn't even smoke or drink or party. He says he never gets drunk. He's faithful to his own wife. Man, he's weird." That's exactly opposite to what weird means. God created us to live a good, wholesome, happy and fulfilled life. The weird ones are those who reject God's way, and go their own unnatural, and sometimes even occult, way!

Now, the biblical explanation of this is very simple, and it makes abundant sense to the human soul. It speaks of a person being "in the Spirit." Now some, looking on from outside of Christian understanding, would say that sounds weird, "walking in the Spirit." What does that mean? Walking around in a trance with your eyes out of focus? There are some who may do that and say they are "in the Spirit," but that is not what the Bible says walking in the Spirit really is. Look at Romans 8:9-10:

> *"But you are not in the flesh but in the Spirit, if indeed the Spirit of God dwells in you. Now if anyone does not have the Spirit of Christ, he is not His. And if Christ is in you, the body is dead because of sin, but the Spirit is life because of righteousness."*

You see, walking in the Spirit is related to whether or not we sin. God created mankind in the original, to naturally not sin. Sin would be unnatural, weird, related to another spirit, not of God. Those whose sins are forgiven, and who live "in the Spirit," draw on the life of God, to live a good, wholesome, healthy, happy and fulfilled life. That's what "natural" is supposed to be. Those who do not follow God's way are the weird ones. Look now at Romans 8:11:

> *"But if the Spirit of Him who raised Jesus from the dead dwells in you, He who raised Christ from the dead will also give life to your mortal bodies through His Spirit who dwells in you."*

Do you realize the implications in all this? When we get back on track, and walk the original 'righteous and strait way' that God intended, we literally have the life of God Himself in us, through His Holy Spirit! That not only gives us life, gladness and health—it's the most UNweird way in the world to live!

Ask yourself a few questions: Which is weird? To live honestly, or to steal and cheat others? Which is weird? To help the poor, or to kick them when they're down? Which is weird? To praise and thank God, or to dress like a Zombie and scream your guts out at a rock concert? Which is weird? To love or to hate? Which is weird? To do good or to do evil?

God is good! And He loves us enough to save us from all our weirdness. The Christian life—living in the Spirit of God—is the most UNweird way of life open to mankind.

Those who call Christians "religious weirdos" do so from the dark side of the moon. I invite them in to the light, to become children of God, and children of the light. It says in Romans 8:14:

> *"For as many as are led by the Spirit of God, these are sons of God."*

The Spirit of God in you is the light you need to walk in the very way that God intended should be normal. If honesty, love, forgiveness and peace are not normal for you, you're weird! Get into God. It's the most UNweird way of life there is on this earth.

Adopted For Life
Romans 8:15-17

When Mary and I adopted our two children, we did not know the future of either of them, other than the fact that our influence would be the greatest single influence in their lives. They might have been left with the other 30,000 children then available for adoption, but we chose them to be ours, and now nothing can ever break that relationship. More about adoption in this study...

I was thinking about my two children, before they were adopted. They were just little three-month-old babies when we took them into our home. But before we knew them, we sincerely desired to have children.

We visited the Children's Aid Society in Toronto and were told that they would be happy to have our application, for a baby boy, on the first occasion. We were told at that time, in 1967, that about 30,000 children were waiting to be adopted.

Research was begun. In a surprisingly short time, a little three-month-old healthy bundle was found. They had matched our background with that of the natural parents. They had researched us. Since we neither drank hard liquor nor wasted money on smoking, they felt perhaps we could handle it—even while living in Africa even on a low salary.

So, we adopted John into our home and into our hearts. He was now a Bombay, and nothing could take him away from us. It was the same with Elaine. Love and acceptance at first sight.

But I couldn't help thinking of the 29,998 that were still without parents. Many of them were beautiful and appealing, but confined in a large room of perhaps dozens of other babies squalling away in rows of basinets. These little ones were without parents; without much promise of a future. Many would go from foster home to foster home, sometimes receiving love and at other times sensing no love at all. Fear would dominate their future.

Most of us were like that before we met our Heavenly Father and were brought into the family of God by simple faith. Look at what the Bible says in Romans 8:15:

"For you did not receive the spirit of bondage again to fear, but you received the Spirit of adoption by whom we cry out, 'Abba, Father.'"

Both John and Elaine can call me "Dad." It is their right. They are mine and I am theirs. They don't have to keep their distance and address me formally as "Father," but are free to use the much more intimate term, "Dad."

Even before they could talk, there was a strong bond. In fact, right in the adoption office when they first placed John in our arms, he smiled. Mary and I were totally "sold." He smiled! Sure, it may have been gas—but at that point I was looking for any excuse to be able to call him "Son." Now read how God accepts us in Romans 8:16-17:

"The Spirit Himself bears witness with our spirit that we are children of God...."

God has gone out of His way to adopt us into His family! And His Spirit is always looking for any sign of love or intimacy from us. He wants us to spend time with Him, to be His sons and daughters.

There's something else that my son and daughter enjoy which they never would have, had they been left out of our family. They inherit everything I have. All that I have is theirs. And God treats us that way too. Let's read on...

"...and if children, then heirs—heirs of God and joint heirs with Christ, if indeed we suffer with Him, that we may also be glorified together."

Both our children went through some of the less appealing times of our life and ministry, both in Canada and in Africa. They sometimes suffered with us, but they also enjoyed the good times. We gave them the best we could.

Ephesians 1:3-5:

"Blessed be the God and Father of our Lord Jesus Christ, who has blessed us with every spiritual blessing in the heavenly places in Christ just as He chose us in Him before the foundation of the world, that we should be holy and without blame before Him in love, having predestined us to adoption as sons by Jesus Christ to Himself, according to the good pleasure of His will...."

My two children did not choose Mary and I as parents. They were too undeveloped in understanding; they were in the dark! We chose them! It was not of works. It was love. It was grace and it was of faith. Just so, God adopts us into His family and kingdom! Wow!

Everything's Not Perfect Yet

Romans 8:18-25

One of the tragedies of childhood is the fact that you have to grow up. The ice cream cone in the hand has to be replaced with a screwdriver because something broke. Life is full of broken things, including hearts, yes, but also some other things like relationships, economies, and ecology. It seems that even some of the glue in our universe is coming loose. It's not long before a sweet and happy child joins the multitude in groaning about life. The whole of creation groans!

Not every child in the world has an easy and happy childhood. But, there are some who do. I was one of them. Although my parents tried to prepare me for some of the harsh realities of life, I was a little reluctant to accept the fact that the older I got, the tougher life seemed to get. I had rather hoped that the innocence, happiness and ease that I enjoyed as a child would last throughout my life.

Part of that was simply becoming aware of problems such as disease, unemployment, debt, and sweat on the personal level; then crime, hunger, death and hate on the social level. To add to these, there are also the horrors of the reality of hate, deceit and war on the international level.

It doesn't take too long for any child who can think, to begin to realize there is a lot in life to groan about.

Yet, at the same time, with the reality of God's provision through Christ, that same child (or you as an adult), can learn to roll with the horrible realities of life—knowing that it is all confined to this life. And for the Christian, the assurance of a glorious future, can keep us stable and steady in an unstable situation. Look at Romans 8:18:

> *"For I consider that the sufferings of this present time are not worthy to be compared with the glory which shall be revealed in us."*

That will be revealed in us when Jesus returns again. But when Jesus Christ came to redeem the world, it was not just the human content of His creation He set about to save. The whole earth, and all creation was God's target for redemption. Those who believe God and receive Jesus as God's gift for the redemption of men, are only an early phase of God's total work of redemption. For the whole of creation has been corrupted by sin, and nature itself is reeling from the blot of evil. But when the Christ of God shall come again, then will be ushered in the full redemption of God's universe. Look at Romans 8:19-21 now:

"For the earnest expectation of the creation eagerly waits for the revealing of the sons of God. For the creation was subjected to futility, not willingly, but because of Him who subjected it in hope; because the creation itself also will be delivered from the bondage of corruption into the glorious liberty of the children of God."

The same perfection which we will enter into when Jesus returns will be shared with the long-awaited perfection of the whole of creation. And just as we groan with the harsh realities of life, so creation groans with the effects of a corrupted universe. Look at the next verse, in Romans 8:22-23:

"For we know that the whole creation groans and labours with birth pangs together until now. Not only that, but we also who have the firstfruits of the Spirit, even we ourselves groan within ourselves, eagerly waiting for the adoption, the redemption of our body."

My soul has been redeemed. But my body is still subject to pain, a thousand diseases, and finally death. I have groaned with pain. I have groaned with despair as recently as the horrendous atrocities in Bosnia. I have groaned in anticipation of that time of total redemption, when Christ will come. That's when our salvation will be complete. That's the day I'm living for!

And that's why as a Christian, I can handle suffering, opposition, criticism, hate, jealousy, and even death. Because none of what life throws at me can compare to the glory which will be revealed in us!

A young child lives in a dream world which does not relate to the harshness of grownup life. Unfortunately, some adults refuse to face the realities of life and insist on their childish dream world accompanying them into adulthood.

But I think the real tragedy is when Christians deny reality, and insist that the qualities of eternity should all be theirs now. The whole package isn't delivered until Jesus returns!

Strength For The Weak

Romans 8:26-30

Good help is hard to get! Even when it comes to prayer, we often look to people who really know how to pray. But even then, their help in prayer is not quite good enough. So where do we go for help? Well, as I said, good help is hard to get, but God's help is easy to get, especially in the matter of prayer.

Did you ever hear the expression, "Good help is hard to get?" It's true! Competence combined with integrity is an increasingly rare commodity. Everyone seems to be out for themselves, and when you do find good help, everyone wants a share of that person. Where real trust is needed, they become the people most in demand to whom to give responsibility.

These kind of people can be given a job, with the confidence that the job will be done in the best way possible. And often, when you really are not sure how to go about solving a problem, they are the ones who come up with good solutions. They are creative, and usually in line for greater responsibility. They are good to have around, because good help is hard to get.

Then, for the Christian, there is the matter of prayer! Most Christians want to know how to pray effectively. They want to know for certain that their prayers are heard, and they want to know for certain that their prayers will be answered. So where do you go for help?

There are scores of books on prayer, and they are good books; most of them very helpful. Let's face it, most of us are weak when it comes to prayer. Well, in this case, good help is easy to find! Look at Romans 8:26:

> *"Likewise the Spirit also helps in our weaknesses. For we do not know what we should pray for as we ought, but the Spirit Himself makes intercession for us with groanings which cannot be uttered."*

God's help is easy to get! There is a dimension in the life of any person who has learned to "walk" in the Spirit, that also strengthens us as we "pray" in the Spirit. It is the privilege of every believer in Jesus Christ, to pray with the help of the Spirit of God. It is effective, creative and powerful, simply because God is involved in the very initiation of the prayer. Now look at Romans 8:27-28:

> *"Now He who searches the hearts knows what the mind of the Spirit is, because He makes intercession for the saints according to the will*

of God. And we know that all things work together for good to those who love God, to those who are the called according to His purpose."

Now, I'm sure that many Christians take comfort and hope from the promise that all things work together for good for those who love God. Yet at the same time, they may find themselves praying for certain things without apparent effect? Why? How can this be? I think the answer is really rather simple.

We pray for things we want! Right? But what verse 27 is saying is that we should learn to pray with "the mind of the Spirit." The Spirit of God has the inside scoop on what God's plans and provisions are for His children. Therefore, when we determine to pray in the Spirit, with the mind of the Spirit, we may find ourselves praying, not so much for what we want or think is right, but for those things which fit into God's plan for us and others.

In 1 Corinthians 14:15, the Bible puts it a little differently. Look at it with me:

"...I will pray with the Spirit, and I will also pray with the understanding."

You really need to read the whole 14th chapter of 1 Corinthians to get the full teaching about praying with the Spirit.

The point is, God knows. He knows everything, and everyone. He knows for whom we should pray. He knows who will become believing Christians, long before they in fact do believe. And he plans for them based on this advance knowledge. Look at Romans 8:29-30:

"For whom He foreknew, He also predestined to be conformed to the image of His Son, that He might be the firstborn among many brethren. Moreover whom He predestined, these He also called; whom He called, these He also justified; and whom He justified, these He also glorified."

The way we pray, both for ourselves and others, depends to a great degree on whether we learn to pray with or in the Spirit. God's help is easy to get!

The Best Love Affair I Have Ever Known

Romans 8:31-39

When spring comes, the hormones in flowers and plants are turned on by the sun, and green growth and beauty once again reign. It's lovely! Human hormones begin to stir, and young men's fancies turn to thoughts of love. It's lovely! But it takes more than merely human hormones to produce love. I want to tell you about the very best love affair I have ever known!

I am told that love is a many-splendored thing. Love bursts forth in the spring-time, since this is the time of year when a young man's fancy turns to thoughts of love. So now the evening streets and parks are populated with young couples, hand in hand, with stars in their eyes, and unhappy hormones skipping through their systems.

Most of them think they are in love, and in fact, some of them really are in love. They would do anything to make the person, whose hand they are holding, happy. They would give anything they are capable of giving, just out of pure love. And that's nice! And that's about as good as a love affair can become: giving, just plain giving, with little or no thought of return.

And that's what real love is! Giving, to please, to help, to protect, to make the loved one as cared for and happy as possible. Most youngsters really don't get bit with this love bug. They get bit with a more monstrous and demeaning bug called lust. They and their unhappy hormones are more interested in what they can get out of this affair than what they can put into it.

Well, the best love affair I ever heard about was when I began to understand how much God loves us when I found out God was available to be 'on my side.' Look at Romans 8:31- 32:

> *"What then shall we say to these things? If God is for us, who can be against us?"*

We all know that God loved the world so much that He gave His Son, Jesus. But did you hear what that verse said, "...how shall He not with Him also freely give us all things?" God loves enough to give us all kinds of things, including His protection. Look at Romans 8:33-34:

"Who shall bring a charge against God's elect? It is God who justifies. Who is he who condemns? It is Christ who died, and furthermore is also risen, who is even at the right hand of God, who also makes intercession for us."

As a child of God, who accepts the love of God in Christ Jesus, you better not mess with me. Because, whoever messes with me, will find himself having to deal with God too. No matter what is done to me, or in what condition I find myself, nothing can squeeze between me and God's love. Read on in Romans 8:35:

"Who shall separate us from the love of Christ? Shall tribulation, or distress, or persecution, or famine, or nakedness, or peril, or sword?"

God's love will sustain, protect and care for me in any place, in any time and in any circumstance. Very few people would ever claim to have such a self-sacrificing love from their own mates. If we could ever really comprehend how much God really loves us, we would probably come apart at the seams. Once you have tapped into the love of God, life suddenly has an anchor that can ride out any storm—victoriously. The last few verses in this chapter are remarkable. Look at Romans 8:37-39:

"Yet in all these things we are more than conquerors through Him who loved us. For I am persuaded that neither death nor life, nor angels nor principalities nor powers, nor things present nor things to come, nor height nor depth, nor any other created thing, shall be able to separate us from the love of God which is in Christ Jesus our Lord."

Have you been persuaded about the power and intensity of God's love? Or have you settled for the wrong concept of love. A love that is conditional, depends on feelings, and even depends on how good you look or act at any given moment. That's the kind of love, which, at the human level, lends itself to failed marriages, and broken friendships. That is not God's kind of love.

God's love is steady, constant, unchanging, unconditional and gives and gives and gives. It's the best love affair I have ever known!

.

No Natural Sons

Romans 9:1-9

We live in a world of blended families. Both my children were adopted. In some homes there are some natural children, and some adopted. In other homes there are children of the mother with children of the father (as blended families). And sometimes there are tensions. But I know of one special family, the best family in the whole world. The only way into that family is by adoption. No natural sons!

There are a lot of cults and religions in the world that make claims to be sons of God. Some claim direct lineage. Others claim to become sons of God through a specific act or ceremony. Yet God's Word makes it very plain that God alone chooses His children. In the case of Israel as a nation, God, in sovereign choice, designated them as His chosen people. Thus, according to the flesh, anyone born a Jew has a certain claim through his common father, Abraham.

The Apostle Paul was a Jew, and could make that claim, according to the flesh by pure physical descent. But God's plan was that more than merely Jews, according to the flesh, should become sons of God. That's why He sent Jesus Christ, His only begotten Son, to open that way of faith. So now, both Jews and Gentiles have the open door of faith to accept Jesus Christ and become sons of God, not according to the flesh, but according to the Spirit.

And the Apostle Paul bemoans the fact that many Jews, even with their historical advantage, did not believe in and accept Jesus Christ. Listen to Romans 9:3-5:

> *"For I could wish that I myself were accursed from Christ for my brethren, my countrymen according to the flesh who are Israelites, to whom pertain the adoption, the glory, the covenants, the giving of the Law, the service of God, and the promises; of whom are the fathers and from whom, according to the flesh, Christ came, who is over all, the eternally blessed God. Amen."*

When God chose Israel as a nation to be His own special people, they had the advantages of being adopted as God's children nationally. They enjoyed the shechinah (or presence) of God in the tabernacle. They were given covenants by God. They were given the Law as a standard of conduct. They served God as His representatives to the world. God gave them promises, and kept them.

It was through Israel that the fathers, Abraham, Isaac and Jacob, came as well as Moses. And most important, it was through these chosen people of God, that our Saviour, Jesus Christ, came; God incarnate; God in the flesh. Is it any wonder that Paul should bemoan the fact that only a few of the many Jews accepted Jesus?

They had the Scriptures! But they could not see past their physical fleshly descent from Abraham to the deeper qualifying factor of faith. Look at the next few verses in Romans 9:6-7:

"But it is not that the Word of God has taken no effect. For they are not all Israel who are of Israel, nor are they all children because they are the seed of Abraham; but, 'In Isaac your seed shall be called.'"

Some of Israel did accept Jesus. All of the disciples, and most of the first believers in the church were Jews. But not all! But just as being born a Pentecostal, or a Greek Orthodox, or a Catholic, does not automatically make you a Christian, so being born a Jew does not make you a child of God. Look at Romans 9:8:

"That is, those who are the children of the flesh, these are not the children of God; but the children of the promise are counted as the seed."

So my being a Christian because my father was Pentecostal is not true. My being a Christian is because of my faith; my personal belief in God! Or you, as a Greek Orthodox, or a Catholic, or a Baptist, or a Presbyterian, does not make you a Christian. God does not have natural sons according to fleshly descent. He has sons supernaturally, through faith. Faith like Abraham's faith. Remember what we read back in Romans 4:3?

"For what does the Scripture say? 'Abraham believed God, and it was accounted to him for righteousness.'"

Our righteousness, or right standing with God, is not inherited. It is received by faith. And it doesn't matter a whit what you have been, or what you are according to fleshly inheritance. You can become a child of God by simply believing in Jesus Christ.

God Is Sovereign
Romans 9:10-18

There once was a time when kings were sovereign. They could do whatever they wanted, to whomever they wanted, at any time and any place. Well, kings are not sovereign any more. Even dictators are limited by the forces of society in these days. But there is One Sovereign left. And He has made a momentous decision that effects every one of us.

As a father, I have certain authority in my home. In our modern world, there are those who would question that, saying that every individual, young or old, has the right to unlimited freedom. If anything has ever convinced me of the error of that position, it is the breakdown in families. Progressively, society's values have broken down as a direct result of that faulty philosophy. Our society has had little respect for any authority in recent years.

Without infringing on individual freedoms of choice, I am still the authority in my home and family. But I am not sovereign. That is, I do not have the authority to do whatever I want, whenever I want, and at anyone else's expense. Only God is sovereign!

And this is a fact that our society might do well to think about. God is sovereign—in power, in authority, in knowledge, and thank God, in mercy! You cannot separate God's sovereignty from His mercy. He can do whatever He wants, at anyone's expense. He can choose to love or hate, to condemn or to have mercy. He is God! The Almighty! Sovereign throughout the universe!

Now, let's read Romans 9:11:

> *"...for the children not yet being born, nor having done any good or evil, that the purpose of God according to election might stand, not of works but of Him who calls...."*

God calls, or elects people to His purposes, even before they are born.

In 1 Peter 1:2 we read about Christians, that they are:

> *"...elect according to the foreknowledge of God the Father, in sanctification of the Spirit, for obedience and sprinkling of the blood of Jesus Christ."*

Long before you were born, God knew you. He knows you from the perspective of eternity. There is no past or present or limits of "time" with God. He is sovereign in knowledge. That's why God can say, based on His advance knowledge of both good and bad people, in Romans 9:13-15:

"*Jacob I have loved, but Esau I have hated.*"

Our immediate reaction is, "How awful!" But, as I said earlier, you cannot separate God's sovereignty from His mercy. In this case, both His sovereignty in knowledge and in mercy is seen. Let us continue to read:

"*What shall we say then? Is there unrighteousness with God? Certainly not! For He says to Moses, "I will have mercy on whomever I will have mercy, and I will have compassion on whomever I will have compassion."*"

God is God! If God decides to show mercy on a person who patently does not deserve any mercy at all, who are we, His creation, to question it. It is said well in Romans 9:16-18:

"*So then it is not of him who wills, nor of him who runs, but of God who shows mercy. For the Scripture says to the Pharaoh, 'For this very purpose I have raised you up, that I may show My power in you, and that My name may be declared in all the earth.' Therefore He has mercy on whom He wills, and whom He wills He hardens.*"

Therefore, if God chooses to show mercy toward anyone and everyone who simply believes in His Son, Jesus Christ, who are we to insist on another approach to God? God has sovereignly decided against good works earning our salvation. He has decided on simple faith. That leaves it open and available to everyone, everywhere, whether Jew, Gentile, Hindu, Muslim or heathen.

In other words, there is no such performance of good in all the world that is good enough to qualify you for faith, nor is there any evil that is so horrendous that it disqualifies you for faith.

God has decided in sovereign grace and mercy to qualify anyone who comes to Him in faith through His Son, and our Saviour, Jesus Christ. It's that simple.

Believe it!

A New People

Romans 9:19-33

What if you were given the power to change one thing in the universe? What would it be? Gravity! Would you like to change that? Or, the colour of grass; would you rather it was pink? Or perhaps the length of human life? Or would you stop all war? Would you like to change the fact that God is sovereign? Some people I've met actually think they have changed God's sovereignty, by not believing it! What sovereign act would you perform, if you were God?

Did you ever have a "What if..." question asked of you by a child? Children are good at asking hypothetical "What if..." questions. "What if I had a million dollars?" or "What if I was able to travel anywhere in the world?" Children love to ask "What if..." questions. It gives free reign to their wild imaginations. A child being disciplined by his father might in a spurt of rebellious courage say, "What if I were bigger than you?" Children's hypotheses are based on hopeful imaginations and dreams.

But there is another form of "What if..." question. It is based on a certain fatalism, an accomplished fact, or an unchangeable situation. Since we're in election mode these days, we could ask, "What if George was elected to Parliament? What can we do about it now?"

Keeping in mind the unchangeable fact that God is sovereign, and that, being God, He can do whatever He likes, Paul asks a "What if..." question. Let's read it in Romans 9:22- 24:

> *"What if God, wanting to show His wrath and to make His power known, endured with much longsuffering the vessels of wrath prepared for destruction, and that He might make known the riches of His glory on the vessels of mercy, which He had prepared beforehand for glory, even us whom He called, not of the Jews only, but also of the Gentiles?"*

In other words, "What if God did show mercy to those who chose Him, and willed the destruction of those who opposed Him?" If God chooses to include some and exclude others in His grace, what have we to say against it? God is God! He can and will do His own will! Thus, when Paul quotes the prophet Hosea in Romans 9:26, and points out that God will claim ownership even of people who are not of the original "chosen people," what do we think we can do about it? Read it with me:

> *"And it shall come to pass in the place where it was said to them, 'You are not My people,' there they shall be called sons of the living God."*

And he quotes Isaiah as saying that only some of the original "chosen people" will be saved. Look at Romans 9:27:

> *"Isaiah also cries out concerning Israel: 'Though the number of the children of Israel be as the sand of the sea, the remnant will be saved.'"*

So we find that God in His sovereign wisdom has decided to neither reject the Gentile world lock, stock, and barrel, nor receive Israel lock, stock, and barrel. He has chosen rather to create a "new people" made up of some from the chosen people of Israel, and some from the Gentile world. And this "new people" are a product of God's mercy and grace. It is not something they have earned or deserved. Those to be included in this "new people" are chosen because of their faith—simply believing God! Look at Romans 9:30-32:

> *"What shall we say then? That Gentiles, who did not pursue righteousness, have attained to righteousness, even the righteousness of faith; but Israel, pursuing the law of righteousness, has not attained to the law of righteousness. Why? Because they did not seek it by faith, but as it were, by the works of the Law. For they stumbled at that stumbling stone."*

And who is this stumbling stone?

Jesus! People don't object to talking about God! Or the Higher Power. They don't object to talking about 'turning over a new page' in life, or making a new start. But when you talk about Jesus saving people, and Jesus giving a person a new life, suddenly you have a stumbling block. Some people just find it offensive to talk about the blood of Jesus Christ cleansing us from sin. Yet God says, in Romans 9:33:

> *"Behold, I lay in Zion a Stumbling Stone and Rock of offense, and whoever believes on Him (Jesus) will not be put to shame."*

I just want the world to know that I, for one, am not ashamed of Jesus. By His sovereign grace and mercy, He saved me.

The Word Of Faith We Preach

Romans 10:1-10

Who keeps promises anymore? Federal and provincial political promises are fresh in our minds. Will they be kept? I suppose it's another 'wait and see' situation. Doesn't anyone honour a promise, a contract, an agreement anymore? Well, I happen to know One who never ever breaks a promise. When He makes a covenant, He keeps it. If He gives you His Word, you can go to the bank with it!

I guess politicians are the only people we somehow excuse for promising to do one thing when they don't have the power to do it, and then not doing it when they do have the power to do it. We somehow let it pass. Political promises are almost expected to be broken.

But what about a contract? What about a contract for politicians; something we could pull out of the file, read it back to them, and then point out their signature at the bottom of the contract? Would that work?

Contracts come in many forms. But often a contract is to hold one particular party to the agreement, although it affects both. Then of course, there are covenants. Covenants are more binding, and hold both parties equally responsible.

Well, God had a covenant with the "children of Israel" as His chosen people. The agreement was that they would live a certain lifestyle and be exclusively faithful to God, rather than mess with the false gods of the tribes and nations around them. And they really tried—sometimes! And they really failed—sometimes! And those among them who had a real zeal for God set about trying to prove it by doing "righteous" things. But God instituted a new agreement to save, not just Israel, but all of us. Paul was concerned because the majority of Israel didn't buy into the "new agreement." Look at Romans 10:1-4:

> *"Brethren, my heart's desire and prayer to God for Israel is that they may be saved. For I bear them witness that they have a zeal for God, but not according to knowledge. For they being ignorant of God's righteousness, and seeking to establish their own righteousness, have not submitted to the righteousness of God. For Christ is the end of the Law for righteousness to everyone who believes."*

Rather than establish their own righteousness by their own righteous acts, Israel (and all of us, under the new agreement, covenant, or contract) simply accept what Jesus did, by faith.

Now faith is talked about a great deal these days, and that's fine. But that basic ingredient of faith that is primary to the whole life of faith is spoken of by Paul as the "Word of Faith." This is not some system of getting prayers answered, nor is it a formula for convincing God to act. Listen to what the "Word of Faith" is according to Scripture. Romans 10:8-10:

> *"But what does it say?* '*The word is near you, in your mouth and in your heart' (that is, the word of faith which we preach): that if you confess with your mouth the Lord Jesus and believe in your heart that God has raised Him from the dead, you will be saved. For with the heart one believes unto righteousness, and with the mouth confession is made unto salvation."*

The Word of Faith is that basic verbal confession of Jesus Christ as Lord and Saviour. It is the expression of belief in the power of the death and resurrection of Jesus. And it is that Word of Faith which, when expressed from the heart, assures us of eternal salvation.

Jesus Himself made it clear that public confession of Jesus as Lord is extremely important. Look at what He said in Matthew 10:32-33:

> *"Therefore whoever confesses Me before men, him I will also confess before My Father who is in heaven. But whoever denies Me before men, him I will also deny before My Father who is in heaven."*

There is no middle ground. And this expression of faith, according to the new agreement God has made with mankind, totally replaces the need to establish your own goodness. It is a total dependence on the goodness of Jesus Christ. A good confession is necessary!

That's why Billy Graham calls people to come forward when making a public confession of their belief in Jesus. That's why we at "100 Huntley Street" have prayer partners who are prepared to hear you confess your faith in Jesus Christ.

Good actions are not good enough. A good confession is essential! And when you do, God keeps His side of the agreement. You're saved!

All Who Believe
Romans 10:11-13

When I was 10 years old, in grade five in school while living in Oshawa, I was shamed publicly by the teacher. I still suspect to this day that she did not know what I was talking about. But on the other hand, I didn't know what she was talking about either. But she was the teacher and I was the student. Therefore, I was the one made to feel ashamed. I sure hope she makes it to heaven because I'd like to revisit that incident. Ashamed without reason!

I vividly remember that incident as a child. Our teacher was instructing us about abbreviations. "Mr." was for mister. "A.M." was morning. Then the teacher asked me a question, right out of the blue. She asked me, specifically me, what the abbreviation "REV." stood for. Well, I knew the answer to that question. It was an abbreviation for the book of Revelation. So that's what I answered, "Revelations, Ma'am." After all, she knew my Dad was a minister, and I would likely know what "REV." stood for.

Suddenly she spoke sternly to me, "Calvin Bombay, I'm ashamed of you! You should know what that means! Your father is a preacher, and you should know! Now what does it mean?"

Well, by then, I was feeling some shame, but I didn't know why. I said again that it was short for the book of Revelation, and I was right of course, even though she may not have known it. What she was after, of course, was that "Rev." was short for "Reverend," and my father was a "Reverend"! Then, when she finally told me, I really was ashamed because I knew that too. Yet its other meaning was what came to my young ten-year-old mind.

I was ashamed, more because of the teacher's scathing remarks than my lack of knowledge.

You know, and I know, that there are times when we are ashamed and we really should not be ashamed!

Sometimes Christians are ashamed to admit their faith in Jesus Christ. They hesitate in telling someone the real reasons they don't indulge in some of the evil habits of the world, as though being a Christian is a shameful basis for purity. Listen to what Paul says in Romans 10:11-14:

"For the Scripture says, 'Whoever believes on Him will not be put to shame.' For there is no distinction between Jew and Greek, for the same Lord over all is rich to all who call upon Him. For 'whoever calls on the name of the Lord shall be saved.'"

Being a Christian means being saved—saved from sin and all its consequences, including the shame of your former lifestyle! As Christians, we have no reason to be ashamed of the faith and the lifestyle that comes as a result of faith in Jesus Christ. It is those who criticise, demean and oppose the righteousness of the Christian life who should be ashamed. Look at what Paul advised a young preacher in Titus 2:6-8:

"Likewise, exhort the young men to be sober-minded, in all things showing yourself to be a pattern of good works; in doctrine showing integrity, reverence, incorruptibility, sound speech that cannot be condemned, that one who is an opponent may be ashamed, having nothing evil to say of you."

And Jesus Himself stated the high importance of being unashamed of Jesus and His Word. Look at Mark 8:38:

"For whoever is ashamed of Me and My words in this adulterous and sinful generation, of him the Son of Man also will be ashamed when He comes in the glory of His Father with the holy angels."

You see, as Christians, we have not only been saved from sin, but from the shame of our sinful past. We need never be ashamed again. And even more important, we should never be ashamed of our stand for purity and righteousness in what Jesus calls "this adulterous and sinful generation." We have the right to be confident and unashamed when Jesus returns again. Look at what the apostle wrote in 1 John 2:28:

"And now, little children, abide in Him, that when He appears, we may have confidence and not be ashamed before Him at His coming."

Christians should never strut with boastful pride because of the fact that their faith won't let them indulge in the evil habits of an evil generation. But on the other hand, Christians have no reason to be ashamed of either Jesus as Saviour, or the style of life that faith in Jesus produces.

Unworthy? Yes! But not ashamed!

Talk About it, But Live It Too!

Romans 10:14-21

Sometimes the lives of Christians are like frost in July to a world that wants good news. When the sun shines, and the life-giving rains fall, and growth and green things are all around us, the thought of a heavy frost is just plain horrible. And just as surely as frost kills tender living plants, so the lives of some so-called Christians can kill a new spiritual life which is responding to the good news of the Gospel.

Everybody is looking for good news. Everyone is looking for good things to happen. For example, when we have periodic changes of government, most people hope for better things to happen. We hope we can believe what has been promised. The word is out and change is in the air. Expectations are tentative, but hopeful. Maybe, just maybe, we have something going that we can really trust, and really believe in.

In this case, we'll have to wait to see.

Then there is this thing that preachers call the Gospel. That means, the "Truth." And it's something that the whole world should hear about, and be given a chance to respond to, believe in, and to receive. But in Romans 10:14-15, Paul asks a very interesting question:

> *"How then shall they call on Him in whom they have not believed? And how shall they believe in Him of whom they have not heard? And how shall they hear without a preacher? And how shall they preach unless they are sent?"*

This is a great missionary paragraph. Many missionaries have preached from these verses, and many have become missionaries in response to these verses. Preachers of the Gospel all around the world are faithfully preaching the glad tidings of Jesus Christ. But in some parts of the world, including Canada, there is a problem.

When good news is spread, it normally lifts the heart. People are happy to hear it. But too often, there are reasons to doubt good news. It's like those bold print SWEEPSTAKE envelopes with your name, saying, "You have just won a million dollars." That seems like good news until you read the fine print that says, "...if (big if), if you have the lucky number we will announce."

A great deal of doubt enters when the fine print is read. In fact, it makes for

81

simple, raw unbelief. And when it comes to the Gospel of Jesus Christ, even though it is in fact good news, not everyone believes it. Look now at Romans 10:16:

> *"But they have not all obeyed the Gospel. For Isaiah says, 'Lord, who has believed our report?'"*

The fact of the matter is that not everyone believes the Gospel of Jesus Christ. The question is: Why don't people believe the truth about Jesus Christ? What is it that raises the questions and doubts in people's minds? Could there be some fine print they are reading?

I believe so! I am convinced that altogether too often, we introduce the fine print into the Gospel story by the way we live as Christians. We do not live up to the standards of faith and behaviour that Jesus calls righteousness. As a result, our lives provide the fine print that turns people away from saving faith. Look for a moment at 2 Corinthians 3:2:

> *"You are our epistle written in our hearts, known and read by all men...."*

What is it people read from your life, and mine? Does it agree with what they hear about the Gospel and what they may read for themselves in the Bible? Is my life-style betraying the faith? This is a hard question, but one every Christian should ask himself.

Yes! Of course! Everyone should hear? Yes! Everyone should believe and receive and be born again through their own personal faith in Jesus Christ! Yes, of course all this is true. And the faith they must have needs to come from the Word of God, the truth of the Gospel, the good news that God has provided salvation through His Son, as it says in Romans 10:17:

> *"So then faith comes by hearing, and hearing by the Word of God."*

That's the bold print, the good news! And it's absolutely true. But too often the fine print that people are reading is what you and I do and say which may contradict the truth of the Gospel. It's not the only reason people don't believe the Gospel, but here in North America it's a major reason!

If you're going to preach it, live it too!

A Remnant By Grace

Romans 11:1-10

As we continue in our study in the book of Romans, we have to face the tough question: Why are some saved, and not others? Why are only some of Israel believing Christians, yet, even though they are God's chosen people, they are untouched by the grace of God? And after all, wasn't it Israel, God's special people, to whom the Messiah was promised? Why some, and not others?

I have a lot of books. In fact, I have literally hundreds and hundreds of books. Somewhere, a long time ago, I got the idea that books were good things. I began to read. I even began to read things that were not assigned to me in school. In fact, I got to the place where I would actually trade good, hard-earned cold cash for a book. I like books. I still have lots of books from when I was a youngster. I could just never bring myself to throw any away. I chose them, I read them, and they were mine. They're still mine. And I'm not about to throw them away. In fact, right now I'm building a study loft upstairs in my barn where all my books can be together.

It may not be the perfect analogy, but I see it as a bit of an example of God and the children of Israel. God chose them. God has dealt with them as a nation, and He's not about to throw them away. Just because some of them don't contribute to God's joy doesn't mean He's going to throw them away. And just because He's in the process of bringing a whole new people into His care and keeping doesn't mean He's lost His love for His chosen people.

Paul talks about Israel in relation to Jesus Christ, God's Messiah, whom many Jews reject. So the question is asked, in Romans 11:1-2a:

> *"I say then, has God cast away His people? Certainly not! For I also am an Israelite, of the seed of Abraham, of the tribe of Benjamin. God has not cast away His people whom He foreknew."*

God has not rejected Israel lock, stock and barrel, since many Jews have actually accepted Jesus as Messiah, and Paul was one of them. I have Jewish friends who have embraced Jesus Christ as Lord. No matter how provoking Israel became to God, God always offered His grace. The prophet Elijah was as angry as a hornet at Israel's behaviour. In his exasperation, he took the matter to God. Look at Romans 11:2b-4:

"Or do you not know what the Scripture says of Elijah, how he pleads with God against Israel, saying, 'Lord, they have killed Your prophets and torn down Your altars, and I alone am left, and they seek my life?' But what does the divine response say to him? 'I have reserved for Myself seven thousand men who have not bowed the knee to Baal.'"

God always has a remnant. In Elijah's day, of all the hundreds of thousands of Jews, there were 7,000 who had remained faithful to God. And, in Israel today, God has his remnant. Look at the next verse, Romans 11:5:

"Even so then, at this present time there is a remnant according to the election of grace."

God's grace responds to faith. In Elijah's day, there were 7,000 who believed in God enough to be faithful to Him. They didn't do anything special, other than remain faithful to God. It was their faithfulness to which God responded. They didn't work for God's grace, they simply believed God enough to not follow after the false god Baal.

Now look at Romans 11:6-7:

"And if by grace, then it is no longer of works; otherwise grace is no longer grace. But if it is of works, it is no longer grace; otherwise work is no longer work. What then? Israel has not obtained what it seeks; but the elect have obtained it, and the rest were blinded."

So, even though Israel as a nation were God's chosen people, it is only those from among Israel who continued to be faithful when God sent His Son Jesus to be their Messiah whom He included in the "elect."

And the "elect" of God are made up of all and any who will believe Him, whether from Israel or from the Gentile nations. The qualification is faith, not the works of the Law. 2 Corinthians 4:4 tells us why:

"...whose minds the god of this age has blinded, who do not believe, lest the light of the Gospel of the glory of Christ, who is the image of God, should shine on them."

So Don't Get Proud!

Romans 11:11-24

We are studying Paul's letter to the Romans. Here in chapter eleven, we find Paul summarizing the doctrinal and theological facts about justification by faith. As a Jew himself, he clears up any misunderstanding about the Jews and their Messiah, and just how Gentiles should think of their own privilege in the Gospel. You'll never really understand God's plan of redemption for the Jews until you begin to understand this chapter.

Christians all around the world seem to have come to a strange conclusion about the Jews. We have somehow concluded that God has forsaken the Jews, and decided to put the believers from Gentile nations front and centre in His plans. And we somehow feel, as Christians from Gentile origins, that we have sort of "perfected the Gospel" and, therefore, the Jews don't figure too strongly in God's plans.

The first thing that must be said about this is that it was not God who rejected the Jews. Rather, it was a Jewish Christian, in frustration of trying to convince them of the Gospel, who turned from the Jews to the Gentiles. And that person, of course, was the apostle Paul. And he had good prophetic grounds for doing so.

But now we find Paul, still a missionary to the Gentiles, pointing out in no uncertain terms that we Gentiles should be appreciative, because of the roots of our Christian faith being deep in the Hebrew religion. Look at what Paul now says in Romans 11:11-12:

> *"I say then, have they stumbled that they should fall? Certainly not! But through their fall, to provoke them to jealousy, salvation has come to the Gentiles. Now if their fall is riches for the world, and their failure riches for the Gentiles, how much more their fullness!"*

Just because the majority of Jews have not accepted Jesus as their promised Messiah does not mean that God rejects them—history, faith and all! After all, God chose them, gave them the Laws and Ordinances, and set them as an example to the whole world. The olive tree still stands, even though some branches have been pruned, and others grafted in. Look at Romans 11:16-18. Remember, Paul was writing here to Gentiles:

> *"For if the firstfruit is holy, the lump is also holy; and if the root is holy, so are the branches. And if some of the branches were broken off, and you, being a wild olive tree, were grafted in among them, and*

with them became a partaker of the root and fatness of the olive tree, do not boast against the branches. But if you do boast, remember that you do not support the root, but the root supports you."

The Christian faith is firmly rooted in Jewish religion and history. It was the rich soil from which the Church of Jesus Christ has grown. The very fact that many Jews did not accept Jesus Christ, causing the unbelieving Jews to be cut off, or pruned—turned out for the good of the Gentiles. For now, by faith and faith alone, believing Gentiles are grafted in to the olive tree.

By the way, the olive tree has always symbolized Israel in the Scriptures.

So, we who are of Gentile origin, find our place in the grace of God. The prophet Isaiah said, and was quoted by Paul in Romans 10:20:

"I was found by those who did not seek Me; I was made manifest to those who did not ask for Me."

We have great reason to rejoice, as Gentiles, that we were included in God's grace, and in God's plans. Reason to rejoice, but not reason to boast. It was all of grace! Paul says in the next few verses, Romans 11:19-21:

"You will say then, 'Branches were broken off that I might be grafted in.' Well said. Because of unbelief they were broken off, and you stand by faith. Do not be haughty, but fear. For if God did not spare the natural branches, He may not spare you either."

Our position in God's grace is nothing to be haughty about, for it is possible to fall from grace. When Paul talks about being justified by faith, in Galatians 3:3, he asks:

"Are you so foolish? Having begun in the Spirit, are you now being made perfect by the flesh?"

Our sins were forgiven through faith, and by God's grace. If we had been able to do it ourselves we would have reason to boast. The fact that there was room at the cross for me will never cease to amaze me and fill me with awe!

Chosen For A Purpose
Romans 11:25-32

When I was a young lad, I didn't always understand the things my Dad did. But normally, I'd find out sometime later why he had done certain things. There was always an explanation available, but sometimes it was just a bit beyond my comprehension. Sometimes God does things that I don't understand, because I guess it's just a bit beyond my human understanding. But God never does anything without a purpose. We may not understand now, but in the sweet bye and bye, we will!

Just north of Toronto there is a factory which makes freezers. They turn out thousands of them. They are distributed and sold all over North America. Some years ago, I went into the factory and asked if they could make a special one for me. I told them that rather than a motor which plugged into Canada's 120-volt, 60-cycle electrical system, I wanted one that ran on 220 volts and 50 cycles.

They looked at me strangely at first, but when I explained my purpose, they began to understand. I wanted to take a 20-cubic-foot freezer to Africa. So I paid the $220 they asked for this special freezer and took it to Africa.

My purpose was to use it for years. Then when I was finished with it, to sell it. And that's exactly what I did. In fact, after many years of use in Africa, I was able to sell it for fives times what I had paid for it originally in Canada. Over all those years, in spite of heavy use, it was more valuable in Kenya used than it was new in Canada. I know a good thing when I see it!

And so does God! Let me explain. God has a purpose in everything He does. I may not be able to comprehend it all or realize all the implications, but God always has a purpose in what He does! When He chose Israel as His special people, and throughout history used them, he had a purpose.

God made some long-range covenants with Israel. He made promises. He also made demands on them. He made use of them on the international scene. God used them as the people out of whom would come Jesus, the Messiah. God made an example of them to the whole world to illustrate His dealings with mankind. And God has an eternal purpose for them as well. They would be more valuable to Him as time went along, like my freezer. And, although it is humanly difficult to comprehend the full purpose of God for Israel, we do know there is a time when God will show how greatly He values them. Read carefully with me now in Romans 11:25-27:

> *"For I do not desire, brethren, that you should be ignorant of this mystery, lest you should be wise in your own opinion, that blindness in part has happened to Israel until the fullness of the Gentiles has come in. And so all Israel will be saved, as it is written: 'The Deliverer will come out of Zion, and He will turn away ungodliness from Jacob; for this is My covenant with them, when I take away their sins.'"*

So, all Israel will eventually be saved! The Deliverer, Jesus, will take away their sin and ungodly rejection of the Messiah. But at the moment, they resist the Gospel. But because of God's promises—His covenant with the fathers of Israel (Abraham, Isaac and Jacob)—God will redeem them. Look at the next verse in Romans 11:28-29:

> *"Concerning the Gospel they are enemies for your sake, but concerning the election they are beloved for the sake of the fathers. For the gifts and the calling of God are irrevocable."*

God does not go back on His promise. So, because of His covenant, He has loved them, and elected them to salvation. Not because they are especially nice people! Not because they have worked their way into God's good graces. But simply because of His mercy and promise.

Most of Israel is disobedient to the Gospel of Jesus Christ, although many, many millions of Gentiles have obeyed the Gospel. And this will finally be an example to Israel. Look at Romans 11:31:

> *"...even so these also have now been disobedient, that through the mercy shown you they also may obtain mercy."*

As Gentiles, we had no covenant with God, and therefore did not deserve His mercy. Israel did have a covenant with God, but rejected His Son, Jesus Christ, and therefore, did not deserve His mercy. That makes us all even before God. Look at Romans 11:32:

> *"For God has committed them all to disobedience, that He might have mercy on all."*

I, for one, am happy about that! God has a purpose in everything He does!

Stained Glass, Unstained People!

Romans 11:33-36

Going into some churches can be a terribly dull experience. Even when people are there, sometimes it sounds like a dull mumble of human voices, just within the range of human hearing. Any sudden or loud noise is frowned upon, both officially, and by meaningful hard glances. And yet when you look at what is pictured in some of the stained glass windows, you can't help but believe it wasn't always so dull in church. Now, let's think about unstained people!

I think churches are interesting structures. You can have everything from a store-front church, with the window painted white, to a great towering cathedral with its stained glass windows. Personally I have been in all kinds of them.

Modern churches are almost clinical in their appearance, with clear bright walls and no dark corners. Some of them don't even have a cross, either on the roof or at the altar. Some older churches are dark, almost dank, with the floors and pews splashed with bright colours from the stained glass windows. Yet those other dark and unseen nooks and crannies seem to hold some secrets.

There is one thing I really love about some of the older churches with stained glass windows. It's the subject matter in the windows. Not just a pattern, but a picture. Not just colour, but life! One of my favourites is a window depicting a number of people in various poses, with their hands and arms raised in praise and adoration to God. It depicts life, real action, real praise you can almost hear!

Where do you suppose they got the idea for those windows? Where would they have seen people who actually raise their hands to God as they praise Him? These windows were in place long before what has become known as the "Toronto Blessing." These windows were designed and in place long before the turn-of-the-century Pentecostal phenomenon. Some of these windows are hundreds and even a thousand years old! Where would people have got the idea that praise to God could be such a visible and noteworthy activity? Good question, right?

Well, first of all, listen to the ecstasy in Paul's praise to God for the plan of salvation, for both Jews and Gentiles, which he had been teaching in the previous verses. It's found in Romans 11:33-36. Observe!

"Oh, the depth of the riches both of the wisdom and knowledge of God! How unsearchable are His judgments and His ways past finding out!"

"For who has known the mind of the Lord? Or who has become His counsellor? Or who has first given to Him and it shall be repaid to him? For of Him and through Him and to Him are all things, to whom be glory forever. Amen."

There is a marvellous ecstasy of the human spirit when we realize both the love and the greatness of God, and when we praise Him for it! It is the most natural thing in the world to raise your hands to God in worship when you praise Him for His wonderful works. Praise to God for His wonderful works goes way back in the history of Israel. Help me rejoice as we read Psalms 9:1:

"I will praise You, O Lord, with my whole heart; I will tell of all Your marvellous works."

But it is not restricted to Israel! Gentiles, too, are encouraged to praise the Lord God. Raise your hands right there at home and help me praise God as we read Psalms 117:1:

"Praise, the Lord, all you Gentiles! Laud Him, all you peoples!"

We have much to praise God for. And those who know the righteousness of God through faith in Jesus Christ, whether Jew or Gentile, have more to praise God for than anyone else on earth. The stains of sin have been removed! So go ahead, and praise our God. Psalms 33:1 exhorts:

"Rejoice in the Lord, O you righteous! For praise from the upright is beautiful."

You are not just a stained glass window depicting something out of the dim past history of the Church. You are a child of God, and beneficiary of the death and resurrection of Jesus Christ. You have a right, and a duty to rejoice in the Lord!

I conclude these thoughts with Paul's instructions to the Christians in Philippi, found in Philippians 4:4:

"Rejoice in the Lord always. Again I will say, rejoice!"

YES! REJOICE! The stains of sin have been removed!

Sacrificing Live Things!

Romans 12:1-2

Most religions of the world practice some form of sacrifice. Some of them are gory. The Christian faith is called upon to make sacrifices too. It can be filled with glory! I'm not talking about some sacrificial financial giving, although there's nothing wrong with financial sacrifice. God is not satisfied with just "things." He wants you, living a life-style that compliments His Name and His righteousness. Gory or glory, you'll likely end up as one or the other.

Many years ago, in various parts of the world, it is a known fact that live babies were thrown into sacrificial fires, as offerings to various gods. These practices are still known to be practiced from time to time.

In fact, it was such a prevalent practice in the tribes around Israel in the times of the kings, that it is mentioned in 2 Kings 17:31:

> *"...and the Sepharvites burned their children in fire to Adrammelech and Anammelech, the gods of Sepharvaim."*

These were not nice people! Yet it is amazing the depths of depravity to which people will go if they can be convinced that their god demands it. Even today, there are some who think that one of the most significant things they can do for God is to ritually abuse their own bodies. Some even do it in the name of Jesus, thinking it is a wonderful sacrifice to make. But that is not what God wants from us. That is simply not in His nature. God wants our attention and devotion certainly, but not out of fear and terror.

In the last few verses of Romans chapter eleven, we read Paul's prayer of praise to God, Who in mercy made salvation available to all men through faith. It is this overwhelming sense of God's love, mercy and care for us that makes us want to do something for God. Sacrifice is often the first thing to come to mind. But the sacrifice of a Christian is not a dead animal, a live child or self-abuse. In Romans 12:1 we read what God will accept:

> *"I beseech you therefore, brethren, by the mercies of God, that you present your bodies a living sacrifice, holy, acceptable to God, which is your reasonable service."*

God will accept our lives lived in holiness and purity before Him and before men. Living our lives for God does not necessarily mean going into either the ministry or a monastery. Living for God simply involves living a life-style which will honour God in all His holiness. That means being honest, fair in all our dealings with others, loving in every situation, kind, good, giving, morally clean, and considering one's own body as the temple of God.

That is in direct contradistinction to the way the godless world lives, and even to the way the world does business. It may appear that this world in which we live (which is becoming smaller and smaller) has some great ways of accomplishing success. But often they are not honest, and justice suffers. That's why Paul goes on to say in the next verse, Romans 12:2:

> *"And do not be conformed to this world, but be transformed by the renewing of your mind, that you may prove what is that good and acceptable and perfect will of God."*

It's easy to assume the methods and worldview of this wicked and adulterous generation. But God offers us a different, more sound worldview which has its origins in the mind of God Himself. That's why Paul can safely tell us to "be transformed by the renewing of your mind...."

God wants you, all of you, body, soul and mind; your body as a life of holy godliness, and your mind to think the way God thinks. And not only should we think the way God thinks, but also come to the same conclusion that God has. How else can we really know what is the "good and acceptable and perfect will of God"?

As you've probably heard Jim Cantalon say, "When you become a Christian, you don't kiss your brains goodbye." As Christians we should learn to think, and I mean think deeply. We have the availability of God Himself to help us think straight, and to come to the right (righteous) conclusions.

So rather than giving a sacrifice of something your hands have done, give Him yourself. Be renewed in your mind. Think like God thinks. And by knowing God better, you will find it easier to know His perfect will.

Practical Christian Living
Romans 12:3-8

I can recall, as a child sitting in class at school, wondering, "When am I ever going to use this stuff they are teaching me?" What I didn't realize at the time was that they were not just teaching me facts in school, they were teaching me to think. And that's where the value of Christian doctrine is found. You may never "use" the theology, but you will know how to think and act as a Christian. Practical Christian living!

In the previous 11 chapters, Paul has been teaching the theology of salvation by faith. In these next five chapters, Paul begins to show how strong basic faith is worked out in the everyday business of practical Christian living.

The first item on Paul's list for practical Christian living is: attitude! One of the most serious mistakes most of us as Christians in the western hemisphere make is the assumption that we are superior—both racially and individually. The Christian faith is, as it should be, the great leveller. We all come to salvation the same way—by a way we could never have accomplished. It is the grace of God that saved us. Paul says in Romans 12:3:

> *"For I say, through the grace given to me, to everyone who is among you, not to think of himself more highly than he ought to think, but to think soberly, as God has dealt to each one a measure of faith."*

Race, background and position mean nothing at all to God. Yet it is distasteful for some Christians in the western world to think of a newly born-again Christian from the slums of Calcutta as their own equal in Christ. But that is the case. Jew or Gentile, male or female, educated or uneducated; it makes no difference to God. He brings us all into His family, every one with a function, but none as superior. Look at Romans 12:4-5:

> *"For as we have many members in one body, but all the members do not have the same function, so we, being many, are one body in Christ, and individually members of one another."*

I have been in over 50 countries of the world, and that includes Africa, Europe and the Orient, and South America. Wherever I have gone, I have met with Christians who are part of the Church of Jesus Christ. We are members one of another. We may have different calls and gifts for ministry from God, but we all are a part of the whole. And as strange as it may seem, I have never yet met a true Christian with whom I didn't have an immediate rapport. I don't mean everyone became a best friend, nor do I mean that I actually liked everyone that much. But I did feel a familial spirit. But we are different, every one of us. Not just in looks or colour, but in the way God has graced us as individuals. Read Romans 12:6-8:

> *"Having then gifts differing according to the grace that is given to us, let us use them: if prophecy, let us prophesy in proportion to our faith; or ministry, let us use it in our ministering; he who teaches, in teaching; he who exhorts, in exhortation; he who gives, with liberality; he who leads, with diligence; he who shows mercy, with cheerfulness."*

It is one thing to be saved by the grace of God, and to respond to His love and forgiveness. To know that the eternal welfare of your soul is settled is basic and wonderful. But the Christian life only begins there. Our whole life on earth from that point onward should be spent in fulfilling the function in the Christian Church to which God has called us, and for which God has equipped us.

The idea that the pastor of your church must carry the whole responsibility for everyone and everything in the church is simply not biblical. We all have specific responsibilities which come with the gifts and abilities God gives us. When we stand before God in eternity as Christians, the judgment of our stewardship will include how we functioned in the Body of Christ, and how faithfully we served.

God's call and gifts are not trivial! Our salvation is not trivial! The attitude we have to our own local church and the Church worldwide is crucial. And as members of the Church, we have non-transferrable duties under God to function smoothly within the fellowship of believers.

And nothing in the world can be more practical than that!

Be One Of The Good Guys
Romans 12:9-21

The Bernardo trial really shocked people and showed to what depths of depravity the human soul can sink. On the surface, looking at Paul Bernardo, he looks like any other innocent and "good" person. But there's a great difference between the human face and the human heart. The fallen nature of man leaves little room for goodness, as all of us who ever had a temptation know! But, with God, good can and does overcome evil.

My little grandson was at our house the other evening when we had a barbecue. It was just about Father's Day. That day was one of those hot and humid days. I was feeling the high humidity and, as a result, was low in patience. Did you ever have one of those days?

Joshua seemed to be in a particularly overactive mode, in spite of the heat. We had four little kittens among the other felines and canines wandering around our feet. Joshua wanted to carry kittens. He'd chase, catch and carry the kittens—holding them too tight, and occasionally dropping one awkwardly. We were all trying to slow him down and and remind him to treat the kittens more gently. Finally his mother, Karen, said, "Joshua, be good!"

Well, it's not really in the nature of a three-year-old to be good. What is in the nature of a three-year-old is to be three years old!

In Romans, the Apostle Paul talks about how we come into the family of God, and how that faith provides entry for all races and peoples. And it is in this family of faith context that he says in Romans 12:9-11:

> *"Let love be without hypocrisy. Abhor what is evil. Cling to what is good. Be kindly affectionate to one another with brotherly love, in honour giving preference to one another; not lagging in diligence, fervent in spirit, serving the Lord."*

It isn't in the nature of natural man, before receiving his new nature in Jesus Christ, to do and be all these nice things. The unregenerate (that means a person who is not yet born again) cannot consistently by nature be good. He can only be what he is: a fallen human soul. Paul is telling us here in very clear terms that we can "Cling to that which is good," because that is part of our new nature in Christ Jesus. But how good are you supposed to get? Well, Paul goes on to say, in Romans 12:14:

"Bless those who persecute you; bless and do not curse."

You have to be pretty good to be able to do that! It's hard enough to stand by and be quiet when you're under fire, but to actually bless those who curse you? That's good...and it's possible! Look at Romans 12:17:

"Repay no one evil for evil. Have regard for good things in the sight of all men."

There's that word "good" again. Christians are supposed to be good. And Paul isn't talking about being good at doing things. He's not suggesting we be skillful. He is talking about doing good and being "good"!

But there are limits, you might say. No one can be perfect, no matter how hard they try. And that's true! Even though we should strive to be perfect, there will be limits as long as we inhabit these weak human frames. And I think Paul recognizes that when he says, in Romans 12:18:

"If it is possible, as much as depends on you, live peaceably with all men."

"If it is possible," Paul states. Sometimes it's just not possible to live in peace with some people. But as much as depends on you, you should put every effort into being a good person.

This is very practical Christian living. It's where the rubber meets the road. This is where theology and Christian doctrine are proven. It is in the relationships and attitudes we have that people will be able to discern whether or not you really have a relationship with God.

In Romans 12:21 we read about the power of good:

"Do not be overcome by evil, but overcome evil with good."

Never overestimate the power of evil. The particularly repulsive evil revealed in the Bernardo trial illustrates just how evil the human heart can become when unchecked by good. But the very fact that a trial was in progress illustrates good overcoming that evil.

A little "good" influence before the fact would have been preferable, and would have kept such evil and depravity in check. Never underestimate the power of good.

Laws are good!

Government And Taxes

Romans 13:1-7

There is a dirty-tongued comedian who is always complaining that he doesn't get any respect, and quite frankly I don't respect him an awful lot myself. But how do you get respect? Does it have to be earned? If so, how can any government be respected, since its members usually don't have time to earn it? On the other hand, should we respect people more for what they represent than for what they are? It's an interesting question, and we'll look at it more closely in this study.

A very funny thing happens to me from time to time. I get respect! I don't think it's necessarily because of who I am, but more because of what I represent. And this respect is not overt. It is something that happens without the person giving it any conscious thought. Well, you may ask, "What in the world are you talking about?" Let me explain:

Several days ago, I was approaching two people in conversation who were using extremely filthy language. They did not notice me at first, but when they did, suddenly their language lost all the filthy four-letter words. They knew I was a minister of the Gospel of Jesus Christ and, out of respect, whitewashed their tongues for a few minutes.

Respect is where you find it. Unfortunately, you don't find it in very many places anymore, even among Christians. Filthy language is hardly the practice of Christians, but often we reveal our lack of respect in other ways. For instance, look at Romans 13:1-2:

> *"Let every soul be subject to the governing authorities. For there is no authority except from God, and the authorities that exist are appointed by God. Therefore whoever resists the authority resists the ordinance of God, and those who resist will bring judgment on themselves."*

Government is of God. Paul is not talking about good government, or bad government. He is talking about good and evil. And government represents law and order. Whether or not we approve of the style of government currently in force is not the question. The crux of this matter is that, as Christians, we must respect the authority of government.

Why? Well, listen to the next few verses, in Romans 13:3-4:

"For rulers are not a terror to good works, but to evil. Do you want to be unafraid of the authority? Do what is good, and you will have praise from the same. For he is God's minister to you for good. But if you do evil, be afraid; for he does not bear the sword in vain; for he is God's minister, an avenger to execute wrath on him who practices evil."

In the last 30 to 40 years, as a society, we have robbed legitimate authority of the respect they must have to function and to control evil in our society. And most Christians have been a party to this.

Most of the general public keep the law simply because they don't want to suffer the consequences. They don't necessarily agree that any particular law is good for society as a whole. They just don't want to go to jail. And that's a pretty good reason for obeying the law. But Christians should have a deeper motive for respecting the law, and Paul states it in the next verse, Romans 13:5:

"Therefore you must be subject, not only because of wrath but also for conscience' sake."

Our obedience to government and law should be a matter of conscience. Christians should be in the front lines of support for law and order. And our support should be total, even to the extent of paying our taxes. Now, I know we can all think of a few dozen horrible instances where our taxes have been used in ways which we find abhorrent, wasteful and even evil. But stop and think for a moment: What would society be without any government at all? Look at Romans 13:6-7:

"For because of this you also pay taxes, for they are God's ministers attending continually to this very thing. Render therefore to all their due: taxes to whom taxes are due, customs to whom customs, fear to whom fear, honour to whom honour."

Those two people respected me for what I represent and stopped their filthy language. Let us respect our governing bodies, not necessarily for what they do, but for what they represent in law and order.

A little more respect for governing authorities would go a long way in bringing about the safe and peaceful society we all want. So, pay your taxes, and pray for those in authority over you.

Pay The Debt Of Love

Romans 13:8-10

Have you ever had the feeling you'll be in debt the rest of your life? Even though I have paid off some debts, I have also incurred new debts. In fact, I do that every month with my credit card. But I was reading a document the other day that convinced me once and for all that I will be in debt until I die. The document? A letter to some people in Rome! The debt? Love! How do you pay a debt of love?

When I got a one-page document from the bank a few days ago declaring and affirming that my mortgage had finally been paid off, my first thought was, "At last, I own my house! Praise the Lord!" My second thought was, "I'm out of debt." Then I remembered the payments on my car, and on Mary's car. And of course there were the several thousands of dollars in my loan account to which I had transferred the balance of my mortgage. And I finally realized, I'm still far from being "out of debt."

But all of these debts are scheduled, and I don't owe the debts until the agreed payment dates each month. If I were to look at the total of the debts I have, it would be scary. But they are sensibly scheduled, so the "scare" is gone, even though the debts are not.

Then, I remembered a debt I would never be able to pay. It's the debt of love. How could I ever repay that kind of debt? God loved me so much, He sent His Son to die for my law-breaking and my sin: to take my punishment on Himself. The only thing I can do is to pay this debt off with my love. And it is a scheduled love.

And I'm not referring to a monthly financial commitment Mary and I have made for the care and education of a child in South America. The schedule for paying the debt of love is daily and, in fact, momentary. Look at Romans 13:8:

> *"Owe no one anything except to love one another, for he who loves another has fulfilled the Law."*

This is not some sort of romantic love which varies with feelings, or with the weather. The only variance with this love is with the opportunity. Love is the deliberate decision to consider others before self. For instance, take a look at Romans 13:9:

> *"For the commandments, 'You shall not commit adultery,' 'You shall not murder,' 'You shall not steal,' 'You shall not bear false witness,'*

'You shall not covet,' and if there is any other commandment, are all summed up in this saying, namely, 'You shall love your neighbour as yourself.'"

Love does not generate adultery, murder, theft, gossip and greed. Those who would otherwise be the subject of such things, when loved, become rather the recipients of kindliness, care and provision. That's the debt of love we owe others. It does them good, not bad. That's why Paul says in Romans 13:10:

"Love does no harm to a neighbour; therefore love is the fulfilment of the Law."

If you were to examine the law, you would have to come to the same conclusion. Laws are in place to protect society from the things people do when they don't love. Laws wouldn't even be necessary if everyone loved others and put others ahead of themselves.

When I do evil things against people, such as theft or gossip, I'm in fact putting them in debt. They have to replace the stolen articles. They have to live down the gossip about themselves. I've made their lives more difficult. But if I do them good, the very opposite is true. Paul, writing to a young preacher in Titus 3:8 says:

"This is a faithful saying, and these things I want you to affirm constantly, that those who have believed in God should be careful to maintain good works. These things are good and profitable to men."

We generally think that it's just criminals who have to pay their debts to society. They must be punished for wrong-doing, that's true. But how much better it would be if we all realized that we all have a debt to society, and that is love.

If God loved us enough to sacrifice His Son for our good, surely we can, out of love, sacrifice something for the good of those around us. And, as I said, this is not like a mortgage debt that is scheduled for once or twice a month. This is a debt that should be paid as the opportunity arises. Look at what Paul concludes in Galatians 6:10:

"Therefore, as we have opportunity, let us do good to all, especially to those who are of the household of faith."

Try it, you'll love it!

Having A High Time

Romans 13:11-14

There are highs and lows in life. Some people reckon they've had a high time, when in fact, they've simply sunk lower. Some Christians flirt with evil, thinking that perhaps they can have a good time without compromising their faith. In fact, some people call themselves Christians and yet seem to live like the devil. What's wrong with people like that? Personally, I agree with a fellow named Paul who said it was high time they woke up!

Have you ever heard the expression, usually after a rather debauching party of some kind, "Well, we really had a high ol' time!"? I actually overheard a young man once say, "We must of had a high time. I can't remember a thing!" What is it that makes you feel you've had a high time in life?

There's another definition of "high time." It's used when a situation has become pressing, and action needs to be taken. You may have used the term yourself from time to time: "It's high time you go out and get yourself a job!" Or perhaps you've heard the expression, "It's high time you quit smoking, or drinking, or whatever...." Well, it's really not quite the expression you'd expect to find in the Bible, but sure enough, that's where it is. Here is Romans 13:11-12:

> *"And do this, knowing the time, that now it is high time to awake out of sleep; for now our salvation is nearer than when we first believed. The night is far spent, the day is at hand. Therefore let us cast off the works of darkness, and let us put on the armour of light."*

It's a little difficult perhaps to believe that Paul would be telling Christians, of all people, to "cast off the works of darkness." But that's precisely what he says. The Christians of Paul's day don't seem any different than Christians today. The second coming of Jesus Christ is far from most Christians' minds. The completion of our salvation is near, and, as Paul says, "the day is at hand"! It's too late to be absorbed with the inconsequential things of this life. It's time we recognized the importance of the days in which we live. It's time to start living like Christians really should be living. Paul goes on to say, in Romans 13:13:

> *"Let us walk properly, as in the day, not in revelry and drunkenness, not in lewdness and lust, not in strife and envy."*

We are living in a day when many people call themselves Christians, but do not live the life of godliness and peace that the Christian faith demands. Take for example the majority in Lebanon who call themselves Christians, but initiate wars and the murder of Muslims. Or, closer to home, look at Paul Bernardo and Karla Homolka who went through Christian marriage vows but didn't live by them at all.

And, perhaps even closer to home, you! You may call yourself a Christian, yet cheat in business, cheat on your husband or wife, drink yourself silly, or curse a blue streak. That's the stuff that Paul says to cast off, as works of darkness. Stop faking it, and get real. Jesus will soon return. In Romans 13:14 Paul goes on to say:

> *"But put on the Lord Jesus Christ, and make no provision for the flesh, to fulfil its lusts."*

It's one thing to understand the theology of the Christian faith, and to know that salvation is by faith in Jesus Christ. But it is really quite another to actually "put on Christ." Instead of your own occasional righteous act, put on the righteousness of Christ so that your faith does in fact produce that new life in Christ which God's grace offers to you.

It's an interesting statement that Paul makes when he says, "Make no provision for the flesh, to fulfil its lusts." It's one thing to be tempted, and to fall into sin. It's quite another to be prepared, just in case a good temptation comes along, so that you can really enjoy the lust of the flesh.

For the Christian, it's not good enough to say, "I'm strong enough to handle any temptation which comes along." The ideal solution for the Christian is to simply avoid anything that has even the slightest propensity for evil.

The Apostle Peter adds his strong words to this in 1 Peter 2:11:

> *"Beloved, I beg you as sojourners and pilgrims, abstain from fleshly lusts which war against the soul."*

Rather than having a high ol' time, perhaps it's high time you awakened to the needs of your soul!

Don't Boast Of Spiritual Strength!

Romans 14:1-4

The Church of Jesus Christ is not a club, but sometimes it sure acts like one: "You can't be a member of our church unless you look like the rest of us." Or, "If you eat carrots, we cannot accept you into membership." Worse still, "You have to be very strong, and at least 5'10" before we can even consider you." Only one qualification is necessary to become a part of the Church, and that is faith. But on the other hand, don't try to foist all your personal petty convictions on everyone else!

When I was a child, a few boys in the neighbourhood decided to have a club for boys only. We were about eight years old, and there were four of us. We got an old wooden crate, and with great difficulty, nailed it to the trunk of a tree, a few feet off the ground. One side of the crate swung open, and we four boys were the only four people in the whole world who knew the secret of how to open that door. Actually, it just swung open, but we pretended that there was a secret method.

Another boy in the neighbourhood wanted to join the club, but he was a sissy in our opinion. We didn't want him in the club, and we totally excluded him. We didn't want to associate with him, because others might think we were sissies, like him.

Well, in a way, the Church of Jesus Christ sometimes acts like that club. We think we have the right to exclude people because of what we perceive as a weakness in them. This is what Romans 14:1 says:

> *"Receive one who is weak in the faith, but not to disputes over doubtful things."*

We are to receive even people whom we consider weak, and spiritual sissies. They have as much entrance by faith into the Church of Jesus Christ as you and I, even if their faith is weak. But Paul warns us not to let their weaknesses become the standards by which we govern the Church. Sound and solid doctrine should be the standard, not petty disputes over trifling matters. Paul takes as his example something that flared up in the early Church. Look at Romans 14:2:

> *"For one believes he may eat all things, but he who is weak eats only vegetables."*

What they should or shouldn't eat became a sore point of dispute. Some tried to bring their personal convictions against eating meat, and force that as the standard. Yet, in the first council of the Christian Church, that decision had already been made. And here was that decision, found in Acts 21:25:

"But concerning the Gentiles who believe, we have written and decided that they should observe no such thing, except that they should keep themselves from things offered to idols, from blood, from things strangled, and from sexual immorality."

The basis for people being accepted into the fellowship of the Church did not have to do with their relationship to food, but their relationship to God. If people have a personal conviction that they should not eat meat, or even carrots for that matter, that is between themselves and God. Or, if another person has a conviction that a good meal must include meat, that also is strictly between his own conscience and God. Look at what Paul goes on to say in the next two verses, in Romans 14:3-4:

"Let not him who eats despise him who does not eat, and let not him who does not eat judge him who eats; for God has received him. Who are you to judge another's servant? To his own master he stands or falls. Indeed, he will be made to stand, for God is able to make him stand."

You see, we are received into the family of God, by God. No man has the right to include or exclude anyone from the company of believers. Faith in God provides direct access. Therefore, we are responsible to God for our own behaviour, not the behaviour of others. Jesus had something to say about this, in Luke 6:37:

"Judge not, and you shall not be judged. Condemn not, and you shall not be condemned. Forgive, and you will be forgiven."

We are not to let the weaker Christians dominate our behaviour when such disputes are brought among us, nor on the other hand are we to judge and condemn anyone for their weakness. We are to forgive.

And when we forgive, we will also be forgiven. This is one of the greatest strengths of the Church! Concern for others, not condemnation!

The Best Holy Days

Romans 14:5-15

It's amazing the number of relationships which have been broken, merely because of a few differences in ideas. The differences may not have been terribly significant in the beginning, but time seems to solidify these ideas into convictions. And it's not too long before these convictions become principles to live by, and in the life of the Church, doctrines. But what is really astounding is that Christians of equal love and dedication to God, and with an equal respect for the Word of God, can become enemies in the area of personal convictions.

So, what's the best time to go to church: Sunday morning, or Sunday evening? Or is Saturday better? And what about Friday evening: isn't that pretty good? Which day of the year is most holy: Christmas, or Easter? Or is every Sunday equally special? Does it make Sunday a more holy day if Christmas falls on a Sunday? Or, on the other hand, who cares? Or perhaps it's better to ask, "Should we care?" To some, this is a very important question, but to the Apostle Paul, he seems to think there are more important matters to consider. Look at Romans 14:5:

> *"One person esteems one day above another; another esteems every day alike. Let each be fully convinced in his own mind. He who observes the day, observes it to the Lord; and he who does not observe the day, to the Lord he does not observe it. He who eats, eats to the Lord, for he gives God thanks; and he who does not eat, to the Lord he does not eat, and gives God thanks."*

In other words, if you have a conviction, stick with it. But don't try to force it on others. Whether it has to do with holy days, or what you eat, that is strictly between you and God. Trying to make other Christians live by your convictions can cause great confusion, and great divisions in relationships and fellowship.

But remember, whatever personal convictions you have and live by in these matters, others (perhaps weaker in the faith) are watching. Sometimes because of spiritual immaturity, personal convictions are puzzling. Yes, our relationship as a Christian is primarily with God, but we cannot pretend that what we say and do has no effect on others. Paul puts it this way in Romans 14:7:

> *"For none of us lives to himself, and no one dies to himself."*

What we do does affect others. What we do not do also affects others. And often, we can become either judgmental or defensive about it. We can hold strong views, and get a bit haughty about our own spiritual position. Take note of Romans 14:10 and 12:

> *"But why do you judge your brother? Or why do you show contempt for your brother? For we shall all stand before the judgment seat of Christ."*

> *"So then each of us shall give account of himself to God."*

Primarily, we are answerable to God, and we will stand before Him one day. And that's well worth keeping in mind at all times. We will give an account of ourselves to God. And we will be judged by God not just for those things we consider right and wrong, such as whether to eat meat, or what day is most holy, but for our effect on the lives of others, even though they may be weak in the faith. Look at Romans 14:13-14:

> *"Therefore let us not judge one another any more, but rather resolve this, not to put a stumbling block or a cause to fall in our brother's way. Yet if your brother is grieved because of your food, you are no longer walking in love. Do not destroy with your food the one for whom Christ died."*

As Christians, strong in the Word, we can develop a strong and faithful relationship to the Lord Jesus Christ and therefore, we can live in liberty. We do not have to subscribe to all the petty rules and controls which others would like to put upon us. We are free. "He whom the Son sets free, is free indeed!" But this does not mean we have license to do anything and everything that comes to mind. Later, in Galatians 5:13, Paul makes a further comment on this!

> *"For you, brethren, have been called to liberty; only do not use liberty as an opportunity for the flesh, but through love serve one another."*

Isn't it interesting how living the Christian life always seems to boil down to some basic truth, such as this: love, and putting the other person first! The essence of Christian living is a conscience clear before God, and a life above reproach in the Church.

The Law Of Love

Romans 14:14-23

I know there are a lot of nit-pickers in the world. People who are always finding fault with the way other people live, or do things. That's often simply the nature of some people. Regrettable, but true! On the other hand, as a Christian, at what stage should I submit to the demands of their consciences? Or should I at all? Am I not free to live my life, accountable to God, without a lot of static from others? I guess it comes down to a very basic question: "What constitutes sin?" Read on if you dare!

When I was a young lad, and belonged to the very exclusive boys' club of four eight-year-olds, we used to play near the crate that we called our club house which was located down by the Oshawa creek. At that age, we thought of it as a great river. I could still take you to a spot where I was convinced I had committed a great sin.

I had found the broken top of a water lock that most city folk have on their front lawns. You probably know what I'm talking about. They are about 3 1/2 inches across, with a square nut in the middle for turning off the water to the house. Well, this one was broken, but it had the words, "Property Of The City Of Oshawa" on it. We kept it in the club house for a few days, then I started feeling guilty. As I read the words "Property of the City of Oshawa," I became convinced that I had stolen property. I had to get rid of it. Finally I threw it into a deep part of the creek. Ah! I was free.

Shortly after this, I learned about finger prints. I was convinced I was going to get caught. Well, here I am, 50 years later, and they still haven't caught me!

I'm slowly becoming convinced that man has constructed a much longer list of sins than God has listed. Romans 14:14-16:

> *"I know and am convinced by the Lord Jesus that there is nothing unclean of itself; but to him who considers anything to be unclean, to him it is unclean. Yet if your brother is grieved because of your food, you are no longer walking in love. Do not destroy with your food the one for whom Christ died. Therefore do not let your good be spoken of as evil."*

The parallel may not be exact, but we often pile guilt on ourselves, or more likely, on someone else, for what we are convinced is a sin. This can apply in eating, in actions or in attitude. But the Christian life is a life of liberty "in God." In this life in Christ, we are free. Free to enjoy life—free to be righteous and just—instead of having our lives all cluttered up with humanly-imposed restrictions: "Don't eat that," "Don't drink that," and so on. Look at Romans 14:17:

"...for the kingdom of God is not eating and drinking, but righteousness and peace and joy in the Holy Spirit."

After over 35 years in the ministry, I have observed that people who are all wrapped up in performance and adherence to all kinds of rules and regulations very seldom, if ever, experience much real righteousness, or peace, or joy in the Holy Spirit. Paul says, in Galatians 5:1:

"Stand fast therefore in the liberty by which Christ has made us free, and do not be entangled again with a yoke of bondage."

We must protect this freedom, and not get all wrapped up in the bondage of rules and regulations. Yet, at the same time, we have an obligation to any brother or sister in Christ who has a weak or immature faith. In other words, we should not let someone else's convictions push us around, but we must push ourselves around once in a while out of consideration for the believers who feel bound by rules. Look at what Paul goes on to say in Romans 14:19-21:

"Therefore let us pursue the things which make for peace and the things by which one may edify another. Do not destroy the work of God for the sake of food. All things indeed are pure, but it is evil for the man who eats with offense. It is good neither to eat meat nor drink wine nor do anything by which your brother stumbles or is offended or is made weak."

So the basic law, once again, that must be emphasized, is love. Love puts the welfare of others first, even if they hold convictions with which you might not agree. If you know by putting your foot out in front of someone, he or she will fall, you just don't do it...unless you have a mean streak!

Be Like Jesus

Romans 15:1-7

Do you remember when you were a child, and a game was to be played? "Captains" were chosen. They in turn chose team members alternately. Usually there was a child with an already battered self-image who was left 'til last. Nobody wanted the weak kid. Well, there's a team to which the weak kid can belong with a full sense of worth, if the Church of Jesus Christ would just pull up its socks, and act like a team!

The Blue Jays are a team. There are times you may wonder, but it's true nevertheless. They are a team, a baseball team. Sometimes they are considered a team in name only because they don't play like a team, in the sense that they don't work together as a well-balanced unit.

Some team members are very strong in one area, but weak in another. Other team members are more than adequate in several areas, but usually have a weakness somewhere. Some can pitch, others can run, hit or snag a ball under the most unlikely situations. And in baseball, it's all very visible. In the past, when they worked well together by majoring on each other's strengths, they brought home the trophy.

The Church of Jesus Christ is a team also. This team, too, is made up of people strong in one area and weak in others. Some Christians are strong in visible areas, but weak in the invisible, and others are weak in very obvious ways, but strong in the unseen areas. In that way, some appear much more than adequate, but others seem almost uselessly weak. This is true in matters of faith as well.

But the big difference between a baseball team and the Church is acceptance and permanency. Great intercessors are not necessarily great preachers, and vice versa. And we must not conclude that greatness of faith is greater than deep personal devotion to God! It's the Church functioning together that makes it great! That's why Paul says, in Romans 15:1-3:

> *"We then who are strong ought to bear with the scruples of the weak, and not to please ourselves. Let each of us please his neighbour for his good, leading to edification. For even Christ did not please Himself; but as it is written, 'The reproaches of those who reproached you fell on Me.'"*

Reproach on any member of the Church is shared by the whole Church, and is also a reproach to the name of Christ. You see, your personal destiny as a Christian cannot be separated from the destiny of the Church. And it is the Church in fellowship and full function together as a team that gives us hope. That hope is based on Scripture, incidently. Look at Romans 15:4:

> *"For whatever things were written before were written for our learning, that we through the patience and comfort of the Scriptures might have hope."*

Patience and comfort! It's interesting that Paul uses these two terms together. We often lose patience with a weaker Christian who just can't seem to keep it all together. And because of our own impatience, we can't sincerely offer comfort and strength to the weaker team member. The Scriptures offer both patience (or steadfastness) and comfort. Now look at what God Himself offers the team, the Church. Romans 15:5-7:

> *"Now may the God of patience and comfort grant you to be like-minded toward one another, according to Christ Jesus, that you may with one mind and one mouth glorify the God and Father of our Lord Jesus Christ. Therefore receive one another, just as Christ also received us, to the glory of God."*

Like-mindedness! With similar goals, similar testimonies, similar devotion to God. This does not imply that we should all be exactly the same in temperament, ambition, methods and strengths. We would then be no better than automatons. We are urged to receive all as members, with all the weaknesses and warts that come with humanity.

It's a very, very, important injunction when Paul says, "Therefore receive one another, just as Christ also received us."

It will glorify God when we accept one another, weak or strong, in just the same way Jesus accepted us. In other words, be like Jesus! This is what gives us the team spirit!

Yes, Accept The Gentiles
Romans 15:8-13

This book, containing all my commentaries from the Book of Romans, is available to all who ask for it. I made a promise. This book would be made available to everyone and anyone who likes me. That was my public promise. What you may not know is that it was also made available to people who hate me. People don't have to sign an affidavit stating they like me; they just have to believe it's available in order to write and ask for a copy. And in a sense, that's what this study is all about! Should I really send a book to everyone who asks?

I have made occasional promises to my son and to my daughter. Some of these promises were expressed to only one of them. But in my mind, since I love them equally, I meant them for both of them.

Let me illustrate what I mean. Mary and I have often said that when we die, our son will inherit whatever we have. We may have said this clearly and openly to our son, but we also include our daughter in whatever inheritance we may leave behind. Our wills, in fact, are written that way. Both our son and our daughter equally inherit whatever we have.

In much the same way, God has made promises to Israel. These have been openly stated and written into the record, the Bible. And because of those specific promises, Jesus came to minister to and redeem Israel. But God's love for the Gentile nations was also provided for them. Here is what Romans 15:8-9 says:

> *"Now I say that Jesus Christ has become a servant to the circumcision for the truth of God, to confirm the promises made to the fathers, and that the Gentiles might glorify God for His mercy, as it is written: 'For this reason I will confess to You among the Gentiles, and sing to Your name.'"*

Paul says this again in 2 Corinthians 1:20:

> *"For all the promises of God in Him are Yes, and in Him Amen, to the glory of God through us."*

So God fulfilled His promise of a Messiah to the Jews, and at the same time, His love and mercy to the Gentile peoples of the world. And this is also a matter of record, so Paul quotes in Romans 15:10-12 from various Old Testament Psalms and Prophets.

"And again he says: 'Rejoice, O Gentiles, with His people!' And again: 'Praise the Lord, all you Gentiles! Laud Him, all you peoples!' And again, Isaiah says: 'There shall be a root of Jesse; and He who shall rise to reign over the Gentiles, in Him the Gentiles shall hope.'"

Thus Paul makes this last and powerful appeal to the Jewish leaders of the church in Rome to accept the Gentiles as full members of the Body of Christ, just as lovingly and openly as Jesus received each of them.

Yet, an amazing fact still faces us today. In our present society, there are people who are the Gentiles for whom Paul was pleading, yet who now discriminate against anyone who doesn't have the credentials and history they have. They somehow feel the promises of God more comfortably fit them than some other ethnic or cultural group.

And they, in fact, do what they would roundly have criticised the Jewish Christian leaders of doing in Rome 1,900 years ago. What other hope is there for any Gentile, or for any ethnic or cultural group for that matter? Jesus is the hope of the whole world. Look for a moment at Colossians 1:27:

"To them God willed to make known what are the riches of the glory of this mystery among the Gentiles: which is Christ in you, the Hope of glory."

Paul then goes on to invoke the joy and peace that God fills believers with as they hope together, and increase in hope. Look at Romans 15:13:

"Now may the God of hope fill you with all joy and peace in believing, that you may abound in hope by the power of the Holy Spirit."

The Apostle Peter shares this same anticipation which is made available to all who believe in the Lord Jesus Christ. Here is 1 Peter 1:3:

"Blessed be the God and Father of our Lord Jesus Christ, who according to His abundant mercy has begotten us again to a living hope through the resurrection of Jesus Christ from the dead."

The inheritance is to all who believe. It's an awful thing when one group of people (or even one person) think they have an exclusive claim to faith. God has given to all men a measure of faith, even to people we think least likely.

Are Missions Still The Mission Of The Church?

Romans 15:14-21

Repetition is a well-proven method of teaching. Right now we are doing it with our dogs, one of whom might be considered too old to learn new tricks. But it looks like it will work, even if it does involve a mild shock from time to time. Do you suppose the Church needs a mild shock and a bit of repetitive teaching to get it back on track when it comes to who can and really should be included in the Church? In other words, are "missions" still valid?

It's not always easy to teach an old dog new tricks. We have a problem with our two female dogs. When they are both turned loose at the same time, they happily run off through the countryside for about eight hours, hunting to their hearts' content. We are trying to teach them to stay home.

We have recently come into possession of a "radio fence" which sends out a radio signal to a receiver in the dog's collar: a sound only a dog can hear. A great deal of training is necessary, and a mild disciplinary shock warns the dog not to cross the invisible fence.

The shock is not necessary after adequate training. Our dogs are taught not to pass through the invisible barrier which is marked with little flags during the training period. The training involves going over and over the same routine with the dogs until it becomes second nature not to pass a certain line on our property

Repetition is a method of teaching, even in the classroom today. Paul knew this method 2,000 years ago. He used it over and over when he taught the Christian Jews that Christian Gentiles were every bit as much a part of the Church as God's chosen people, the Jews. Here is what he says in Romans 15:14-16:

> *"Now I myself am confident concerning you, my brethren, that you also are full of goodness, filled with all knowledge, able also to admonish one another. Nevertheless, brethren, I have written more boldly to you on some points, as reminding you, because of the grace given to me by God, that I might be a minister of Jesus Christ to the Gentiles, ministering the Gospel of God, that the offering of the Gentiles might be acceptable, sanctified by the Holy Spirit."*

Up until now, Paul's reasoning was doctrinal. Now, he takes on a slightly different approach. He states that God has done some rather remarkable miracles by the power of the Spirit of God, through Paul, in bringing the Gentiles into obedience to the Gospel. Look at the next few verses in Romans 15:17-19:

> *"Therefore I have reason to glory in Christ Jesus in the things which pertain to God. For I will not dare to speak of any of those things which Christ has not accomplished through me, in word and deed, to make the Gentiles obedient—in mighty signs and wonders, by the power of the Spirit of God, so that from Jerusalem and round about to Illyricum I have fully preached the Gospel of Christ."*

In other words, the Gospel has been preached to the Gentiles. The Gentiles have responded in faith. God has confirmed their faith with signs following. Now it is time to conclude that the Church of Jesus Christ is truly universal, and that the Gospel needs to be preached beyond the confines of Israel as a nation. The Gospel is for the world. Paul uses his own methods as an example to follow. Look at Romans 15:20-21:

> *"And so I have made it my aim to preach the Gospel, not where Christ was named, lest I should build on another man's foundation, but as it is written: 'To whom He was not announced, they shall see; and those who have not heard shall understand.'"*

Once again, the universality of the Church of Jesus Christ is emphasized. And even though the announcement of the coming of the Messiah was to the Jews, He, (Jesus), came also for those "To whom He was not announced." And they will understand. That is the mission of the Church—missions—reaching the "whole" world with the truth of the Gospel. No one should be left out; no one should be excluded.

How many times will the Church need to be reminded and reminded, and reminded again, that the work of the Church is missions. Some churches have left missions out, having become old and established. Well, you can teach an old dog new tricks, even though it may take a bit of a shock!

The Preacher Plans His Itinerary

Romans 15:22-28

I used to hear a saying that goes like this: "The best laid plans of mice and men often go awry!" And that's true. Did you ever have a plan that back-fired? What about the plans of a preacher—an evangelist? He's a man of God. Shouldn't he be able to make plans that work? Well, strange as it may seem, the more plans Paul seemed to make, the less they worked. For years he had wanted to go to Rome to preach, but when he did arrive in Rome it was as a prisoner. And he had plans to go to Spain, but there's no record that he ever made it! Let's travel with Paul a bit!

Paul had been so busy preaching the Gospel to the Gentiles, while at the same time trying to convince the Jews. As a result many of his travel plans had been delayed. He had covered the whole Middle East it seemed, when he stated that he had gone everywhere from Jerusalem to Illyricum.

Like most evangelists, Paul needed to make some plans for his next place of ministry. Paul was no different. In fact, he was the great example of a missionary evangelist. When he had no place left to go in one area, he would lift up his eyes, to look on new fields! He writes in Romans 15:22-24:

> *"For this reason I also have been much hindered from coming to you. But now no longer having a place in these parts, and having a great desire these many years to come to you, whenever I journey to Spain, I shall come to you. For I hope to see you on my journey, and to be helped on my way there by you, if first I may enjoy your company for a while."*

I have no idea whether or not Paul ever made it to Spain. But I'm quite sure if he was alive today, and was able to get to Spain, he would be pleased at what has begun to happen there. Paul had a strong desire to spread the Gospel in Spain, and he intended to drop by Rome in the process. But first he had a special duty to perform in Jerusalem. Look at Romans 15:25:

> *"But now I am going to Jerusalem to minister to the saints. For it pleased those from Macedonia and Achaia to make a certain contribution for the poor among the saints who are in Jerusalem. It pleased them indeed, and they are their debtors. For if the Gentiles have been partakers of their spiritual things, their duty is also to minister to them in material things."*

He had a bag of money, collected by the believers in Macedonia and Achaia, for the needs of the people in Jerusalem. And Paul says this is proper. For the believers in Jerusalem had ministered to them spiritually. It was therefore quite proper for them to minister back to them in material ways. That is how the Church should work. Not just internationally, but locally as well. Paul reiterated this same principle in 1 Corinthians 9:11:

> *"If we have sown spiritual things for you, is it a great thing if we reap your material things?"*

It is quite biblical and proper that if this ministry, "100 Huntley Street," has ministered to you at a spiritual level, we should legitimately expect that you would minister to the material needs of this ministry. So, we find Paul acting simply as a courier, delivering these funds to Jerusalem on behalf of the donors in Macedonia and Achaia. After that, he repeats his travel plans in Romans 15:28:

> *"Therefore, when I have performed this and have sealed to them this fruit, I shall go by way of you to Spain."*

Paul's travel plans always seemed only tentative. They were always subject to change without too much notice. You will remember in the book of Acts how he planned to go into Bithynia, but the Holy Spirit forbade him. Other times he was chased out of one town by angry Jews. His plans were exceeding tentative.

And, as we know from the last few chapters of the book of Acts, Paul eventually made it to Rome, but not in quite the style he had probably hoped. He arrived in Rome as a prisoner of the State. But that did not repress Paul. He continued to preach, teach and write his letters to the churches.

There is a major lesson in this, for all of us. We don't have to wait until we get fully equipped, fully educated, and into place, whether Africa or wherever, to get on with the cause God has called us to. The simple matter of the fact is that the Gospel must be shared with all men everywhere, as soon as possible. Sometimes "plans" don't come to pass!

We'll Handle Our Problems Through Prayer

Romans 15:29-33

When plans don't work out, what is our first reaction? To blame someone? Try manipulating the situation to force the plans to work? When it looks like trouble on the horizon, what do you do? Do you look for another horizon? Do you try to solve all the problems out of your own wisdom? Or, do you do as the first travelling evangelist did—ask for prayer? Prayer requests are quite all right, you know. We get a lot of them in the mail. And we have prayer requests too. Here is what I think are the most important ones.

The first time I went to Rome, I was travelling with Mary on our way to Africa as missionaries. We happened to be there over New Year's Eve. And I must tell you, the Romans seem to enjoy New Year's Eve. We stood in awe as old rejected furniture was thrown out of windows into the streets at the stroke of midnight, with no regard to what it might fall onto. It was bedlam. Well, we were two young, innocent missionaries going to Africa, and we had our own ideas as to how relaxed and nice the trip should have been. But we were travelling at God's call, with His peace.

When the Apostle Paul was planning his trip to Rome, he also had some ideas of how his trip should go. Here is Romans 15:29:

> "But I know that when I come to you, I shall come in the fullness of the blessing of the Gospel of Christ."

Well, as we know, he arrived as a prisoner of the State—hardly what you might call the "fullness of the blessing of the Gospel of Christ"! Except that it was exactly that. You see, Paul didn't look at his problems as insurmountable. He had come to the place where he simply prayed about it and asked others (in this case, the Christians of Rome) to strive with him in prayer. Let us read Paul's request for prayer in Romans 15:30-32:

> "Now I beg you, brethren, through the Lord Jesus Christ, and through the love of the Spirit, that you strive together with me in prayers to God for me, that I may be delivered from those in Judea who do not believe, and that my service for Jerusalem may be acceptable to the saints, that I may come to you with joy by the will of God, and may be refreshed together with you."

117

Everyone needs prayer! Paul needed prayer. And I need prayer. David, Lorna, Jim and all of us on this program need prayer. Those who minister the Gospel need prayer—real earnest prayer. Because there are enemies. And I don't say this lightly. There are those who do not believe the Gospel, and have even convinced themselves that the Gospel of Jesus Christ is a danger to our society. Some of them have nasty minds and nasty plans. They actually wanted to kill the Apostle Paul, and tried more than once. That's why he asked the saints to pray that he "may be delivered from those in Judea who do not believe."

But protection was not the only prayer request Paul had. He also requested prayer that the Gospel, the Word of the Lord, would be received quickly. Look at what he wrote to the people in 2 Thessalonians 3:1:

"Finally, brethren, pray for us, that the Word of the Lord may run swiftly and be glorified, just as it is with you."

Paul realized the fact that he was a weak human being. He mentions another prayer request that every preacher should have. It has to do with life-style, holiness, integrity and ethics. It's mentioned in Hebrews 13:18:

"Pray for us; for we are confident that we have a good conscience, in all things desiring to live honourably."

We have the same three prayer requests. There are other prayer requests, such as that God will give us wisdom, the resources we need, His clear guidance, and so on. But these three stand out:

1. God's covering and protection on our lives.
2. That the Word of God will have good success: souls rescued!
3. That we will live honourably in the sight of both men and God!

And the last verse in Romans 15:33 speaks to all of us:

"Now the God of peace be with you all. Amen."

In spite of the society in which we live; in spite of the economy; in spite of the universal uncertainties; and in spite of the murder and mayhem around us— we can have peace in God Himself.

When the God of peace is with you, you can have confidence, no matter what happens around you!

Preaching Is Not A "One-Man Show"

Romans 16:1-16

When a strong personality is front and centre all the time, it is easy to conclude that a Christian ministry is a "one-man show." Yet, that is literally never the case. Some may be seen more prominently than others, but the unseen and sometimes the unnamed are often the strength and foundation of a ministry. It was true in Paul's day and it's true today! Whether a primitive travelling evangelist like the Apostle Paul, or a modern television evangelist like David Mainse—if it wasn't for friends, very little would happen!

I have met thousands of people over the years, and sometimes I find it just a little embarrassing when someone greets me with fond familiarity, yet I don't have a clue where I may have met them. I look at them closely, trying desperately to place them in some familiar setting. But more often than not, I need more than just a hint. I have thousands of people with whom I have some acquaintance, but among them there are those who I do remember in detail, usually for a special reason.

Some are friends from my youth. Others, I may have spent a day or two with in a fishing boat, or perhaps years working with in Africa. There are others who have made special impressions because of what they have done, either in personal or ministry support. Some have made significant contributions to my spiritual welfare. Some live in Oshawa, Nairobi, Kenya, and yes, at least one lives in Rome. There are others in Russia, Thailand and throughout Europe and Africa.

And when I look at the 16th chapter of Romans, it has the ring of familiarity. There are people of special significance, either to the Apostle Paul or to the work of the Gospel. Look at the first two verses, for instance. Romans 16:1-2:

> *"I commend to you Phoebe our sister, who is a servant of the church in Cenchrea, that you may receive her in the Lord in a manner worthy of the saints, and assist her in whatever business she has need of you; for indeed she has been a helper of many and of myself also."*

Phoebe is mentioned only once in Scripture, but was obviously a significant deaconess in the early church in Rome. Others were even more familiar and personally significant to Paul. There was a husband and wife ministry team who risked their own lives for Paul. Look at the next two verses, in Romans 16:3-4:

> *"Greet Priscilla and Aquila, my fellow workers in Christ Jesus, who risked their own necks for my life, to whom not only I give thanks, but also all the churches of the Gentiles."*

Then there were some with good Gentile Roman names who were Christians even before the Apostle himself, who shared a prison cell with Paul somewhere, some time! Look at Romans 16:7:

> *"Greet Andronicus and Junia, my countrymen and my fellow prisoners, who are of note among the apostles, who also were in Christ before me."*

These are some of the people who make up Paul's life and ministry. Some with shared experiences, others with shared resources. One woman apparently shared so much of herself and her resources that Paul referred to her as "mother." It may have been personal care after one of Paul's numerous beatings. It may be that she was an intercessor for Paul. It may be that she was a major financial supporter. And she had a godly son too. Look at Romans 16:13:

> *"Greet Rufus, chosen in the Lord, and his mother and mine."*

No minister of the Gospel operates in a vacuum. There are significant people who help form, support, and guide any preacher. And, just for your information, such people are very deeply appreciated. Without them, the ministry would be a lonely and difficult occupation. And whether it's me, or David Mainse, or the Apostle Paul, our affection for such people is strong.

Now, I'm not the kissy-squeezy type, but I do go along with what Paul says to all these people. After all, we're family. He says in Romans 16:16:

> *"Greet one another with a holy kiss. The churches of Christ greet you."*

This is not some sort of passionate embrace Paul is promoting, but a family-like greeting of personal respect and affection. And I just want you to know, that I feel the same way Paul does about the family of God. If anyone on this planet is worth a kiss or a hug, it's a fellow Christian!

Don't bother hugging a tree today, but it might be nice to hug a Christian!

Careful, Not Everyone Is Constructive!

Romans 16:17-20

It's not always easy to recognize truth. This is especially true if you haven't spent very much time pursuing truth. So, when the next exciting evangelist comes to town, and he stirs up a lot of controversy, how are you going to know whether he's legitimate or not? The Scriptures have a lot to say about these things, and false prophets are no more in the past than you are. Here's how Paul says we should treat them!

Occasionally people write to me asking about a certain church or organization, and even once in a while about individual preachers. Sometimes there are questions of veracity, or perhaps doctrinal standards. And the truth of the matter is, unfortunately, we sometimes do find people parading as spiritual leaders, but whose life-style or doctrine does not measure up to scriptural standards.

People often ask me about someone I have never heard of, or about an organization which is being questioned of which I have no knowledge. I will conclude, in passing, that I do not measure a person's doctrine or ethics by what I hear about them from others. I try to restrict myself to first-hand experience before I pass an opinion on someone.

But, since the Bible does give us some clear standards of spiritual leadership, we must, at times, challenge people whose lives or teachings are out of sync with the Word of God. This does not necessarily mean they are heretics, but simply that they need reproof and correction. And we all are obligated to try to lovingly help them live or teach in accordance to biblical standards.

Yet in all this, there is a very small number of people who live a lie. They preach an exciting message, and often have great personality. But they are divisive, and their message is usually opposing someone, or when examined, is a strange deviation of accepted biblical truth. They do not mind offending people either. In fact, they can be extremely offensive to others.

At the end of Paul's letter to the Romans, he sounds an urgent note about such people. Read it with me in Romans 16:17-18:

"Now I urge you, brethren, note those who cause divisions and offenses, contrary to the doctrine which you learned, and avoid them.

For those who are such do not serve our Lord Jesus Christ, but their own belly, and by smooth words and flattering speech deceive the hearts of the simple."

Such people are self-serving, and normally they trap only people who do not think for themselves, but respond emotionally to flattery and smooth words. For this reason, we should study and know God's Word so that we cannot be easily deceived. Simple people find themselves obeying these people, rather than the Gospel. Paul says to avoid such people. Stay away from them. Don't have anything to do with them. Send their mail back unopened.

And although Paul was pleased that the Roman Christians were obeying the Gospel, he was concerned that they not dabble in bad things, but that they put their intellectual and spiritual wisdom into what is "good." He says in Romans 16:19:

"For your obedience has become known to all. Therefore I am glad on your behalf; but I want you to be wise in what is good, and simple concerning evil."

As we will see in the next study, obedience to the Gospel is the basic essential Paul wants the Roman Christians to practice. It is in the steady practice of godly living and a living faith in Jesus Christ that we have the assurance of final and complete victory. And let's face it, none of us are so spiritually healthy that we can live above reproach and in perfect victory all the time. It takes God's grace to face much of life. That's why Paul says in Romans 16:20:

"And the God of peace will crush Satan under your feet shortly. The grace of our Lord Jesus Christ be with you. Amen."

Now that sounds like the end of the letter. But it's not! Paul still has something on his mind that he wants to say, and it's important. We'll look at that in the next study, the final one.

To Him Be Glory

Romans 16:21-27

This is our last study in Paul's letter to the Christians in Rome. But I hope that it is just the beginning of a new interest in this particular New Testament book for you. In the last few verses of the letter, you can sense the spiritual ecstasy with which Paul contemplates the wonder of God's grace, that He would spread His love around so lavishly on a world that deserves anything but love. Join me as we take a last lingering look at Romans in this series.

In our studies in Romans we have discovered the solid basis of the doctrine of "Salvation by Faith" which Paul has clearly taught from both Old Testament prophecy and the death and resurrection of Jesus Christ. We see clearly that no one, regardless of their origin or former lifestyle, is excluded from the family of God (the Church of our Lord Jesus Christ) when they put their personal faith in Jesus, the Son of God. The gates of heaven are open wide to all men, everywhere, Jew and Gentile alike.

At what appears once again to be the end of his letter, Paul sends greetings from quite a number of Christians with him when he dictated the letter. Tertius was his secretary; Timothy, his fellow-worker; Erastus, the city treasurer; and Gaius, his host in whose house the church came together. Others also are mentioned. Then Paul says, in what appears like the conclusion of the letter, in Romans 16:24:

> *"The grace of our Lord Jesus Christ be with you all. Amen."*

That's the same thing he said in verse 20. But Paul's mind is filled with the wonder of God's grace, and with the might and magnificence of His great love for mankind. So he puts into words his great benediction, words that are often repeated from pulpits around the world. These words express the overwhelming blessing of God to mankind through the Gospel of our Lord Jesus Christ. Here is Romans 16:25-27:

> *"Now to Him Who is able to establish you according to my Gospel and the preaching of Jesus Christ, according to the revelation of the mystery kept secret since the world began but now has been made manifest, and by the prophetic Scriptures has been made known to all nations, according to the commandment of the everlasting God, for obedience to the faith—to God, alone wise, be glory through Jesus Christ forever. Amen."*

In Paul's opening remarks of Romans, back in 1:4, he used exactly the same words he now uses here at the end of this very long letter: "...for obedience to the faith." That is the declared purpose of Paul: to explain the simplicity of the Gospel, and to bring people of all and every origin into obedience to the faith. That also is my declared purpose in life as a minister of the Gospel of Jesus Christ.

If it were in my hands to make a decision for you, I would immediately bring you into obedience to the Christian faith, for your own good. But I cannot do that! I have found it quite a task in life to bring myself into full obedience to the faith. I have human weaknesses and face challenges to my faith that are quite enough for me to handle. There have been times early in my ministry when I wasn't even walking as closely to the requirements of the Gospel as I should have. But as I live, and grow in God, my obedience to the faith also grows. I am not the man I used to be. I never want to be again the man I used to be. But what I am, I am by the grace of God. And I still have a long way to go. And it gets better all the time!

My challenge to you, either as a Christian, or as a person who has perhaps been skirting the edges of the Christian faith, is to look at Romans again. Read it through again now—personally, slowly, thoughtfully and prayerfully.

Most national revivals have been accompanied by a new emphasis on the truths of Romans. Revitalization in your own spiritual life will take place as you take to heart the ageless depths of this book.

My comments through Romans have been an attempt at highlighting some of the truths found in it. The fact is, the resources of truth in this book are far beyond my ability to expound. You can find them for yourselves, for in every verse there is a gem: a priceless truth which can change your life, your mind, your relationship to God and everyone around you.